# INFORMATION SYSTEMS DEVELOPMENT

Paul Beynon-Davies

# M
## MACMILLAN

First published 1989

Published by
MACMILLAN EDUCATION LTD
Houndmills, Basingstoke, Hampshire RG21 2XS
and London
Companies and representatives
throughout the world

Laserset by
Ponting–Green Publishing Services, London

Printed in Great Britain by
Billing & Sons Ltd, Worcester

British Library Cataloguing in Publication Data

Beynon-Davies, Paul
    Information Systems Development.–(Macmillan
    computer science series).
    1.  Information systems
    I.  Title
    001.5

    ISBN 0-333-48034-1
    ISBN 0-333-48035-X Pbk

# *Contents*

For Gillian

# *Preface*

Most of the conventional material on information systems development is deterministic in the sense that it imposes some prior framework on the use of the techniques available. The present book is designed to be as flexible or non-deterministic as possible. It provides a series of relatively discrete, self-contained sections or notebooks on important topics in the field. It therefore largely leaves it up to readers of the book to impose their own determinism.

This mode of presentation will, I feel sure, be of greater benefit to persons running courses in systems development than the traditional approach tied to one methodology. It will also, I feel sure, more clearly suit the purposes of computer professionals with a desire to know more about particular topic-areas. This applies not only to those persons who perhaps do not wish to work within the confines of any one methodology, but also to those looking for a more detailed treatment of specific subject-areas that are perhaps not well covered in the documentation of an existing methodology.

The book is divided into four major parts. The first part provides an initial discussion of some of the background issues involved in the need for, and development of, a systematic discipline of information systems development. We discuss the software problem, the project life-cycle, the development of structured analysis, design and programming, and relational database systems.

The second part discusses the major techniques of contemporary systems development. It describes a tool-kit out of which most of the contemporary methodologies have been built: data-flow diagramming, data dictionaries, normalisation, entity–relationship diagramming, entity life-histories, structured walkthroughs and structured design. Each of these sections contains three parts: a detailed discussion of the technique, a small example, and a set of problems for further study.

The third part of the book discusses a number of tools designed to aid or enhance the software development process. We cover the present generation of computer-aided software engineering (CASE) tools, most notably integrated project support environments and fourth-generation languages. We also highlight the role that knowledge-based systems may have in the development environments of the future.

In the final part we discuss issues relating to the organisation of systems development. That is, how some of the tools and techniques previously covered take their place within a general methodology or 'philosophy' of systems development.

Information systems development has become almost exclusively associated in Britain with one particular government standard methodology which goes under the title of structured systems analysis and design method (SSADM). A recent paper has however criticised the trend towards developing competing methodologies – a trend that we might label as 'methodolotary'. Benyon and Skidmore (1987) believe that the methodolotary trend is hampering progress towards successful systems analysis. They consider it is unlikely that a single methodology can prescribe how to tackle the great variety of tasks and situations experienced by the systems analyst.

There are, however, alternatives to the 'waterfall' model of systems development as characterised by frameworks such as SSADM. In the fourth part of the book, therefore, we also consider rapid prototyping and James Martin's suggestion for an encompassing discipline of information engineering, based around the explicit use of CASE tools.

The concluding chapter considers some of the possibilities for the future of information systems development. We organise our discussion in terms of one central premise, that information systems development is primarily a case of conceptual modelling. This premise encourages us to discuss three areas of modern computing that are contributing new tools, techniques and philosophies to this endeavour: artificial intelligence, database work and programming languages.

# 1 Introduction

## The software problem

Over the last 20 years hardware performance has increased by an order of 100. In the same period, software performance has increased only by an order of 10. This is usually described as 'the software problem', 'the applications backlog', 'the software bottleneck' or 'the hardware–software gap' (Boehm,1981).

The software bottleneck is really the high-level representation of a whole series of smaller problems:

1. Users cannot obtain applications when they want them. There is often a delay of years
2. It is difficult, if not impossible, to obtain changes to systems in a reasonable amount of time
3. Systems have errors in them, or often do not work
4. Systems delivered do not match user requirements
5. Systems cost much more to develop and maintain than anticipated

## Software engineering

Many solutions to these problems have been proposed. One of the most influential, probably because it is the most comprehensive, has been to try to cast software development as an engineering exercise.

> Software engineering is the practical application of scientific knowledge in the design and construction of computer programs and the associated documentation required to develop, operate and maintain them. (Boehm, 1976)

This rather general definition captures the all-encompassing nature of the term software engineering. Software engineering is an attempt to found the entire project life-cycle in a systematic approach to software development.

The above definition, is however, somewhat vague. It contains at least one term, namely 'scientific knowledge', which is subject to a number of different interpretations. A more practical definition of software

1

engineering might therefore be:

> The systematic application of an appropriate set of techniques to the whole process of software development.

This definition concisely presents the three important principles of software engineering:

1. A set of techniques is used to increase quality and productivity
2. The techniques are applied in a disciplined, not a haphazard, way
3. The techniques are applied to the whole process of software development, that is, over the entire life-cycle of a project.

One of the important themes of software engineering is its emphasis on a clear *structure* for software development. This is usually contrasted with the traditional *ad hoc* approach to software development, an approach that is seen as being the major contributory factor to the software problem.

## Structured programming, design and analysis

In response to a dissatisfaction with the traditional *ad hoc* approach to software development, three more rigorous areas of computing have been developed (King, 1984):

1. Structured programming: the attempt to construct a disciplined programming methodology based upon firm notions as to an appropriate syntax for procedural programming languages. This was the emphasis of the late 1960s and early 1970s in the computing world
2. Structured design: the discipline of building hierarchical systems of modular software. This was the emphasis of the mid to late 1970s (Yourdon and Constantine, 1979)
3. Structured analysis: an attempt to separate the logical from the physical description of information systems. The emphasis of the early 1980s (Weinberg, 1980).

These three areas, traditionally seen as sub-disciplines of software engineering, have now become accepted practice within conventional systems analysis and design. They correspond roughly to the three major stages of the software development process: analysis, design and implementation.

This book concentrates on systems analysis and design. Because of the interdependent nature of software development, however, we will necessarily have to touch upon aspects outside this fuzzy domain. For instance, we will discuss the context of information as an organisational resource, and some of the tenets underlying the construction of well-designed programs.

## The software development process

Structured software development is usually seen as being made up of a series of well-defined stages, with well-defined inputs to each stage, and well-defined outputs from each stage (see figure 1.1).

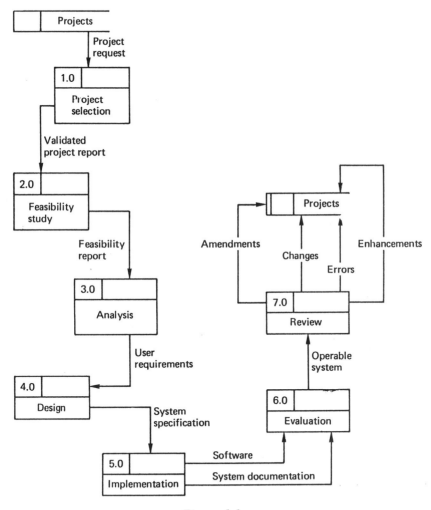

*Figure 1.1*

In large organisations, there are usually a large number of requests for applications systems. To handle such a diversity of applications formally, most enterprises engage in some form of project selection process. The purpose of such a selection process is to identify the most suitable applications for development in terms of organisational objectives.

The primary mechanism of the project selection process is the project selection committee. The project selection committee does not examine each project in detail. This is the responsibility of the feasibility study. Here, a systems analyst, or team of systems analysts, identifies the initial framework for the application, and investigates whether it is feasible to tackle the project given the available organisational resources. The end-result of the feasibility study is the feasibility report. This is presented to the relevant users who offer their opinions. These opinions may then be fed back into the feasibility study which produces a revised report, and so on.

In a sense, the project selection process and the feasibility study are two 'filters' at the beginning of the development life-cycle. Project selection is a coarse-grained filter. Its objective is to reject those projects which are clearly unsuitable. The feasibility study is a fine-grained filter. Its objective is to reject projects on more detailed grounds (see figure 1.2).

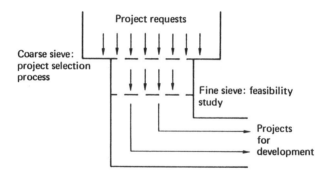

*Figure 1.2*

Once the users are satisfied with the feasibility report, it is fed into the definition phase. This is the systems analysis proper. The end-result of this phase is the user specification or user requirements document. Elements within the requirements document are continually reviewed with end-users until they are satisfied that the requirements adequately describe their needs.

The requirements document is a logical view of the proposed system. This must be turned into a physical or implementable view of the system through the process of design. The end-result of this design process, the systems specification, is again reviewed with users until all interested parties are happy with progress.

Once the completed design is ready, it is used to produce the application system. Programmers are given specifications for the various modules of the system, and proceed to program them in the language and on the hardware chosen for the implementation. Another important product of the implementation phase is documentation which must fully describe the system, both for technical staff, and for the end-user.

The system, once written and tested, must be subject to a critical evaluation phase. This primarily means comparing the system produced with elements of the requirements document to check that it has achieved its aims.

Once the system is in operation, it is usually subject to a whole series of user reviews. Such reviews usually generate a continuous series of further project requests – amendments to the existing system, suggestions for new systems etc,. which feed back again into the project selection process.

Software development is often referred to as a cycle for two major reasons:

1. It is subject to a whole series of small iterations surrounding the user reviews, both within phases and between phases
2. A system is seldom 100 per cent complete. Users will continually want errors in the system corrected, parts of the system changed, or major extensions added. Software maintenance is therefore a critical factor which should influence all aspects of the development process.

This 'waterfall', linear, or 'loopy linear' model of software development is the one most often adhered to within the information systems development community. Recently, however, a more iterative or incremental method of systems development has been proposed. This participative approach, which is usually called prototyping, or sometimes rapid prototyping, is considered in Chapter 16 (Dearnley and Mayhew, 1983).

**The major themes**

Contemporary information systems development can thus be characterised in terms of five major themes:

1. The emphasis on structure. That is, as we have already discussed, the software development process is made up of a series of well-defined procedures which act on well-defined inputs to produce well-defined outputs. It is therefore a framework which constrains the software development process in directions that have been shown to produce better systems. For instance, it has been shown that clear and well-considered structure lead to more maintainable systems (Yourdon, 79)
2. The emphasis on data. That systems analysis and design should

concentrate on data rather than process. This means that the prime area of concern is the data needed to support organisational behaviour. The procedures undertaken in any enterprise are seen to be by-products of, or reliant upon, organisational data. This emphasis encourages a global integrated view of organisational data

3. The emphasis on user and peer group participation. All stages of the software development process are subject to some form of user and peer group review. This is particularly important in the analysis and design stages. User involvement has been proved to produce better systems in terms of a closer match between user requirements and finalised systems. Peer group reviews of the products of the development process are a necessary validation mechanism (Yourdon, 78)

4. The emphasis on logical modelling. That is, the importance of building an initial model of a system which is not tied to any specific implementation plan. In other words, structured systems analysis and design enforces a necessary 'fire-wall' between the analysis and design stages in development. Analysis involves primarily producing a documentation of user requirements. Design involves turning such requirements into an implementable plan

5. The emphasis on graphical presentation. Most of the techniques used in structured systems analysis and design are graphical in nature. This results from the view that one of the major problems of traditional software development is the problem of communication. A problem of communication exists between the systems analyst and the end-user, between the systems analyst and the programmer, and between the systems analyst and management. Diagrams are a proven method of enhancing communication; they are easier to understand by everyone involved in the development of software. They are also easier to manipulate, and represent information far more concisely than the written page (Martin and McClare 1985).

## Data-directed development

Structured systems analysis and design constitutes data-directed development. Data-directed analysis and design emphasises two opposing but complementary views of data: the dynamic view, and the static view.

1. The dynamic view emphasises the importance of data flow. That is, how data moves through the system, and is transformed by the various processes making up the information system.

2. The static view emphasises data structure. That is, how data is or should be organised in a system in order to support organisational processes.

Two major techniques have been used to support these views: data flow diagramming and entity–relationship (E–R) diagramming. These two methods form the core of our discussion in the techniques section.

The other techniques to be discussed, such as data dictionaries, entity life histories and structure charts, are really means for enhancing this dynamic duo. For instance:

1. Data dictionaries are a method of enhancing and extending the documentation of data flow.
2. Entity life histories are a method for connecting up the activities or events represented on a set of data-flow diagrams with the entities on a set of entity–relationship diagrams.
3. Structure charts are fundamentally a means for transforming a dataflow diagram into something closer to a programmable structure – a hierarchically organised set of program modules.

## Databases and database management systems

Given the emphasis on data in modern information systems development it is not surprising that perhaps the greatest influence on the approach in recent years has been the development of databases and database management systems. In particular, one database model has laid claim to supremacy, at least in methodological terms. This is the relational database model to be discussed in some detail in chapter 2. Without a basic understanding of this model, the chapters on normalisation, E–R diagramming, and indeed the whole question of information resource management cannot be properly understood.

## Insufficient improvements from structured techniques

As has been mentioned, the main hope for improving productivity over the last two decades has been the application of structured techniques. Recently however, it has been claimed that few installations have benefited from an increase in productivity of greater than 50 per cent from the application of structured techniques alone (Martin, 1984). This has led many people to direct attention to a whole range of other issues which are considered to be further sources of productivity enhancement.

In this book, we shall address a number of such issues. First, we shall address the way in which relational databases and relational database management systems (RDBMS) have not only influenced the application of structured techniques, but are influencing the whole future development of computing. Using RDBMSs as a core we shall then address a whole range of environmental issues that are moulding the software development process. For instance, we shall consider the use of prototyping, fourth-generation languages (4GLs), integrated project support environments and knowledge based systems. Each of these topics will be cross-referenced so that in the concluding chapter we can make some sensible predictions as to the future of the activities of systems analysis and design.

**Information systems engineering**

At the start of this chapter we described how software engineering has been proposed as one of the most comprehensive solutions to the software problem. In recent years, a yet more sophisticated solution called information engineering or information systems engineering has been proposed: (see for example Martin, 1984):

> The term software engineering refers to the set of disciplines used for specifying, designing and programming computer software. The term information engineering refers to the set of interrelated disciplines which are needed to build a computerised enterprise based on data systems. The primary focus of information engineering is on the data that are stored and maintained by computers and the information that is distilled from these data. The primary focus of software engineering is the logic that is used in computerised processes (Martin, 1984).

Information engineering builds itself on a number of premises:

1. That data lie at the centre of modern data processing.
2. That the types of, or structure of, data used in an organisation do not change very much.
3. That given a collection of data, we can find an optimal way to represent it logically.
4. That although data are relatively stable, the processes that use such data change fast and frequently.
5. That because the basic data types are stable, whereas processes tend to change, data-oriented techniques succeed if correctly applied where process-oriented techniques have previously failed.

Although Martin tends to contrast information engineering with software engineering, the author believes that it is more appropriate to cast information engineering as an overarching discipline which encompasses not only traditional software and systems engineering issues, but a global concern with the management of information in organisations. This is more realistic in a number of senses:

1. It emphasises the important part that structured techniques have in the construction of data systems.
2. It makes clear the desirable development of software on the firm foundations of information-engineered data models.
3. It allows for the modification of traditional software development methodologies by new fourth- and perhaps fifth-generation technology.
4. Information engineering represents a concern not only with the computerised aspect of information systems, but also the other important 'manual' aspects which go into making any information system.

## Automation of analysis and design

Figure 1.1 represents the software development process as a data-flow diagram, a technique to be discussed in chapter 6. This is useful in the sense that it emphasises the nature of software development as an information system in itself. The production of software under the aegis of a structured methodology is subject to a series of relatively well-defined processes and well-defined inputs to and outputs from each process.

This recursive or incestuous view of software development has been effective in influencing a minor revolution in the analysis, design and implementation of information systems. It has led to the view that software development, considered as an information system, should be subject to and benefit from the same sorts of automation that characterise everyday information systems. This revolution has been given a number of names of which perhaps the most popular is computer-aided software engineering (CASE).

In chapter 12 we discuss one aspect of CASE, the notion of an integrated project support environment or (IPSE). This is really a systems analyst's workbench: an information system for producing information systems. It is made up of a cohesive set of facilities to support and enhance the use of most of the techniques that we shall be discussing in the techniques section. The ideal IPSE has facilities for:

1. Project control
2. Document production
3. Diagramming
4. Inter and intra-project communication

IPSEs are normally firmly linked with the idea of a fourth-generation language. A fourth-generation language is a higher-level language than conventional programming languages such as COBOL, Pascal or FORTRAN. The ideal fourth-generation language would employ a declarative as opposed to a conventional procedural approach to systems development. This will be discussed in chapter 13.

One of the conclusions we shall come to is that systems analysts are not simply software engineers or information engineers, they are also knowledge engineers. The fundamental problem of systems analysis is how to represent some subset of organisational knowledge in a computational medium. This is the issue of knowledge representation – a well-studied topic in artificial intelligence. It is for this reason that we include a discussion of knowledge based systems in our tools section. The analyst needs better tools for knowledge representation, and knowledge based systems offer one such tool.

**Formal methods**

One of the major emphases of structured approaches to software development is the attempt to improve the correspondence between the specification of a problem and the implementation of a solution in terms of some computer software. Making a specification more precise in this manner usually means searching for ways to make unambiguous statements about what a program or system should achieve.

Because the most unambiguous language available to us is that of mathematics, a recent trend has been towards more mathematical and hence provable methods of system description. These are the so-called 'hard' methods of formal specification, a brief overview of which is given in chapter 18.

In a sense, techniques such as data-flow diagramming and E–R diagramming are formal in that they use a notation founded in some systematic rules for the specification of user requirements and software design. Because they lack the rigour of formal languages, however, such techniques fall within the 'soft' category of formal methods.

**Conclusion**

A lot will necessarily be left unsaid in the pages to follow. Although, for instance, we touch upon notions of project management throughout the book, we do not discuss this well-documented field in any detail. Similarly, we say very little about important implementation issues such as structured testing or human factors.

The aim of this book is simply to give the reader some in-depth understanding of the important topics within contemporary systems analysis and design. It also attempts to use this material for discussing some of the important issues for the future of systems analysis and design.

# 2 Databases and Database Management Systems

## Introduction

When organisations first began to use computers they naturally adopted a piecemeal approach to software development. One manual system at a time was studied, redesigned and transferred on to the computer. This approach was necessitated by the difficulties experienced in using a new and more powerful organisational tool.

The piecemeal approach has the drawback, however, of producing a number of separate systems, each with its own program suite, its own files, and its own inputs and outputs. As a result of this:

1. The systems, being self-contained, do not represent the way in which the organisation works, that is, as a complex set of interacting and interdependent systems.
2. Systems designed in this manner often communicate outside the computer. Reports are produced by one system, which then have to be transcribed into a form suitable for another system. This proliferates inputs and outputs, and creates delays.
3. Information obtained from a series of separate files is less valuable, because it does not provide the complete picture. For example, a sales manager reviewing outstanding orders may not get all the information he needs from a sales system. He may, for instance, need to collate information about stocks from another file, used by the organisation's stock control system.
4. Data may be duplicated in the numerous files used by such different systems in the organisation. Hence, personnel may maintain information similar to that handled by payroll. This creates unnecessary maintenance and the risk of inconsistency.

## Databases and Database Management Systems

Because of the problems inherent in the piecemeal approach, it is nowadays considered desirable to maintain a single centralised pool of organisational data, rather than a series of separate special-purpose files. Such a pool of data is known as a database.

It is also considered desirable to integrate the systems that use this data, around a piece of software which manages all interactions with the database. Such a piece of software is known as a database management system (DBMS).

**The database**

A database may therefore be defined as a collection of structured data, shareable between different parts of an organisation's information system (see figure 2.1). A database is characterised by a number of properties:

1. Program–data independence. Most traditional applications are data-dependent. This means that the way in which the data is organised, and the way in which it is accessed, are both dictated by the requirements of the application. Moreover, knowledge of data organisation and access are built into the applications' logic. Hence it is impossible to change the storage structure or access strategy without affecting the application. In contrast, databases, because of their sharing function, must be data-independent. Data independence might be defined as the immunity of applications to changes in the storage structure and access strategy of data (Date, 1986).

2. Data integration. This implies that a database should be a collection of data which has no redundancy, that is, no unnecessarily duplicated or unused data (Howe, 1983). If we had a payroll system and a personnel system for instance, we should make great efforts to avoid duplicating information about company employees which is used by both such systems.

3. Data integrity. This associated property implies that when maintaining data we can be sure that no inconsistencies are likely to arise in the database. Suppose, for instance, we maintain a customers file and sales file in our database, both of which contain a customer number. Integrity means that if we wish to change a customer's number for some reason, we have to do so in affected records in the sales file, as well as in affected records in the customers file.

4. Separate logical and physical views of data. The major idea behind the database concept is the attempt to model the natural or logical structure of data and separate this out from the exigencies of any particular implementation of such data on a physical device.

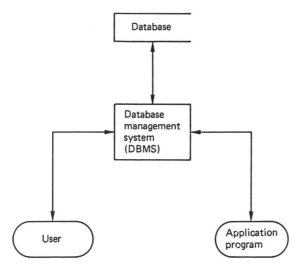

*Figure 2.1*

**The database management system (DBMS)**

A database is composed of a collection of shared data. A DBMS is a collection of shared facilities used to access or maintain a database. The following facilities are found in most DBMSs:

1. Interface between end-user and database
2. Interface with application programs
3. Allocation of storage to data
4. Facilities for file processing – indexing, sorting, etc.
5. Provision for security
6. Statistics on data usage

**Multilevel architecture**

The four major properties of a database discussed above are best achieved by creating a multilevel architecture for the DBMS. At its simplest, the DBMS might be divided into three general levels:

1. Internal level. The level involved with the way in which data is actually stored.

2. External level. The level closest to the way in which different users and/or application programs 'view' the database.
3. Conceptual level. The level which provides a mapping between the internal and external levels. If the external level is concerned with defining individual user's views of the database, the conceptual level may be thought of as defining the community or organisational view of the database.

## Database models

A database model concerns the general structure of how data is organised. There are generally held to be three fundamental database models (see figure 2.2).

Hierarchical

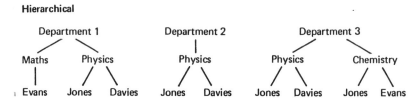

Network

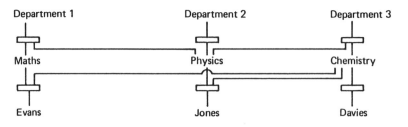

Relational
----------

Department                      Course

Dept. no.      Dept. name       Course ID      Course name

| Dept. no. | Dept. name | Course ID | Course name |
|---|---|---|---|
| 1 | Department 1 | M | Maths |
| 2 | Department 2 | P | Physics |
| 3 | Department 3 | C | Chemistry |

Student

Student no. Student name

| | |
|---|---|
| 246 | Evans |
| 324 | Jones |
| 355 | Davies |

Department/course        Course/student

| Dept no. | Course ID | Course ID | Student no. |
|---|---|---|---|
| 1 | M | M | 246 |
| 1 | P | P | 324 |
| 2 | P | P | 355 |
| 3 | P | C | 324 |
| 3 | C | C | 246 |

*Figure 2.2*

1. The hierarchical model. This model is a direct extension of commonly used data-processing methods. Basically, data is organised hierarchically in relationships of ownership. For example, in an educational database, departments might be said to 'own' courses, which in turn 'own' students. The major problem with this approach is that it encourages data redundancy. Hence, in our example, if a number of departments collaborated in running a course, the course information would have to be duplicated for each participating department.
2. The network (CODASYL) model. This extends the concept of hierarchy into the concept of a network. Each entity or record within the database is joined to other relevant entities by a system of pointers. Using our educational example again, the three departments, three courses, and six students represented in figure 2.2 are linked together in a complex network. The major problem with the network model is that the programmer or end-user needs to know a great deal about how to 'navigate' through the database to extract information (Bachman, 1973).
3. The relational model. The relational model organises data in one uniform representation. Everything in a relational database is represented in the form of two-dimensional tables related together by common attributes.

**Conclusion**

Databases and DBMSs are important for modern information systems development because they encourage the development of an integrated policy for organisational data. Such policy more clearly reflects, or models, the organisation as being a set of interdependent subsystems. In chapter 17, for instance, we will discuss how information resource management is a discipline devoted to this exercise in integration.

Of the three database models discussed, the relational model has certainly achieved a dominance, at least in methodological terms. Because of its influential nature we devote the next chapter to a detailed discussion of this model.

# 3   *Relational Database Systems*

## Introduction

Most people involved in commercial computing have heard of the terms *relational database* and *relational database management systems*. Why have they achieved this degree of importance? There are four main reasons:

1. The term 'relational' is so fashionable that it influences the buying strategies of large commercial organisations.
2. Any new DBMS is almost guaranteed to attempt to fulfil at least some of the requirements of the relational model.
3. The relational model is ideally placed to influence the future strategy of commercial computing; for example, in the area of distributed database systems, knowledge based systems, etc.
4. The relational model was influential in instigating a number of techniques which are now essential components of structured systems development.

In the present chapter, we shall first attempt to describe what is meant by the relational model and explain some of the factors which go into making it such an interesting development, in terms of both of current and future commercial computing.

## The relational data model

According to Codd, the creator of the model, the relational data model consists of at least three components (Codd, 1985):

1. A collection of data structure types, that is, the basic building blocks of a database.
2. A collection of operators.
3. A collection of general integrity rules.

Let us examine each of these in turn.

**Data structures**

The relational approach to data is based upon the realisation that files that obey certain constraints may be considered as mathematical relations, and hence that elementary set theory (and more importantly predicate logic) may be brought to bear on the various practical problems of dealing with data in such files. The relational model was drawn up as long ago as 1970 by Dr E. F. Codd, at that time an IBM scientist (Codd, 1970). Since his first publication, the model has become so influential that any modern database or DBMS worth its salt uses the term 'relational' somewhere in its publicity material.

All data in the relational model is organised into two-dimensional tables called *relations*. The rows of such tables are generally referred to as *tuples*, because the term has a generally more precise definition than 'row' or 'record'. Likewise, columns are usually referred to as *attributes* of the relation. In this and subsequent chapters however, we shall use the everyday terms *table*, *row*, and *column* interchangeably with their more technical counterparts.

Relations are tables constrained in the following way (see figure 3.1):

```
        Relation-name          Salesforce
                               ----------


        Attributes

        Salesman_no    Name      Sales_area    Target

               01      Jones     London        20000
               03      Brown     Edinburgh     15000
               02      Smith     Paris         25000
Tuples         04      Stevens   Sweden        40000
               06      King      New York      25000
               05      Harris    Glasgow       10000
```

*Figure 3.1 A simple relation*

- All entries in a column must be of the same kind.
- All columns must be assigned distinct names.
- The ordering of columns is not significant.
- Each row in a relation must be distinct, that is, duplicate rows are not allowed in any one relation.
- Each column/row intersection (cell) in a relation should contain a

single value. This is often referred to as an 'atomic' value. In other words, multiple values are not allowed in any one cell.
• The ordering of rows is not significant.

The constraint detailed above, that each row must be distinct, means that each relation must have a so called *primary key* – an attribute or combination of attributes whose value uniquely identify the rows. A relation may also contain so-called *foreign keys*; these are keys that reference other relations in a database. The important point, however, is that interconnection between data in a relational database is represented in one and only one way – through common attributes. Hence in figure 3.2, there is a clear relationship between the *Salesforce* and *Customers* table represented by the common attribute Sales_Area.

```
Salesforce
----------

        Salesman_no      Name      Sales_area      Target

            01          Jones     London          20000
            03          Brown     Edinburgh       15000
            02          Smith     Paris           25000
            04          Stevens   Sweden          40000
            06          King      New York        25000
            05          Harris    Glasgow         10000



Customers
---------

        Customer_ref     Customer_name    Sales_area

            04          Ericsson         Oslo
            01          Knight           London
            03          Maurice          Paris
            02          Klein            New York
            06          Burt             London
            05          Harris           Edinburgh
```

*Figure 3.2 A simple relational database*

**Operators: the relational algebra**

Relational systems are designed to operate on whole files (relations) of data, rather than on the individual records (tuples) or fields (attributes) within a file. The manipulative part of the relational model consists of a set of operators known collectively as the *relational algebra*. The result of any retrieval operation in the relational algebra is always another table. Each operation takes either one or two relations as its operands and produces a new relation as a result. The three fundamental operators in the relational algebra are:

- *Selection*: creates a subset of all rows in a table (figure 3.3).
- *Projection*: creates a subset of all columns in a table (figure 3.4).
- *Join*: combines two tables on a common column (figure 3.5).

Figures 3.3, 3.4 and 3.5 demonstrate the application of some statements in the relational algebra on the tables in figure 3.2.

```
Select from salesforce where target <= 15000 -> Low_target

Low_target
----------
```

| Salesman_no | Name | Sales area | Target |
|---|---|---|---|
| 03 | Brown | Edinburgh | 15000 |
| 05 | Harris | Glasgow | 10000 |

*Figure 3.3 An example of selection*

```
Project name, target from salesforce -> Targets

Targets
-------
```

| Name | Target |
|---|---|
| Jones | 20000 |
| Brown | 15000 |
| Smith | 25000 |
| Stevens | 40000 |
| King | 25000 |
| Harris | 10000 |

*Figure 3.4 An example of projection*

```
Join salesforce and customers on sales area -> result
```

Result

------

| Salesman_no | Name | Sales area | Target | Customer_ref | Customer_name |
| --- | --- | --- | --- | --- | --- |
| 01 | Jones | London | 20000 | 01 | Knight |
| 01 | Jones | London | 20000 | 06 | Burt |
| 03 | Brown | Edinburgh | 15000 | 05 | Harris |
| 02 | Smith | Paris | 25000 | 03 | Maurice |
| 04 | Stevens | Oslo | 40000 | 04 | Ericsson |
| 06 | King | New York | 25000 | 02 | Klein |

*Figure 3.5 An example of a join*

## Integrity rules

Integrity refers to the accuracy or correctness of data in a database. It normally means protecting the database from authorised users by the application of some set of rules which are designed to maintain the logical consistency of the database. In relational databases two such rules are of primary importance:

- *Entity integrity*: the rule that in any relation there must always be a primary key, and that no part of the primary key may be null. What we are really saying here is that there must always be a unique identifier for each row in a table.
- *Referential integrity*: the rule which states that a foreign key must either be null or the value of the primary key of an associated table. The reasoning behind this rule is as follows: if a row of relation Products contains a foreign key Supplier_no, then a row for supplier Supplier_no should exist in relation Suppliers. If the foreign key is null, then we must be certain that no row corresponding to Supplier_no exists in Suppliers.

## A relational database management system

In the above discussion we have described some of the components that go to define the characteristics of a relational database. Of equal importance, however, is that piece of software which manages all interaction with the database by end-users and application programs – the so-called relational database management system (RDBMS).

Many of the characteristics of an RDBMS have already been discussed in the previous chapter. All we shall say here is to reiterate that one of the primary goals of any DBMS is to achieve something called program/data independence – the necessary separation of data from the application programs that use them.

This facility is important in the sense that it allows us to evolve our database without worrying about the impact that such evolution might have on our application programs. For example, a RDBMS should allow you to add a new column to a table, change the format of a data item, or even add a new table to the database without the need to change any of the software that accesses the database.

There are a number of ways in which program/data independence is achieved in a RDBMS. Most such mechanisms, however, revolve around the use of an entity known as the *system catalogue*, *database catalogue*, *database directory* or *data dictionary*. In essence, the system catalogue is the place where all the table definitions for a particular system reside. Hence, a primitive system catalogue for the sales database presented earlier might look as follows:

```
Tables                          Columns
------                          -------


Tabname   Colcount  Creator     Tabname    Colname        Type

salesforce   4      PBD         salesforce salesman_no    char(2)
customers    3      PBD         salesforce name           char(20)
                                salesforce sales_area     char(20)
                                salesforce target         num(5)
                                customers  customer_ref   char(2)
                                customers  customer_name  char(20)
                                customers  sales_area     char(20)
```

The system catalogue supports program/data independence in the sense that any changes made to the structure of the database are made to the system catalogue not to the data themselves.

A variant approach to this problem is through the concept of a *View*. A view is a virtual table, or a 'window' on the set of real tables which make up the database. For instance, in SQL (short for Structured Query Language, the emerging standard language interface for RDBMSs, – see chapter 13), a view on the *Salesforce* relation might be defined as follows:

```
CREATE VIEW LONDON_SALES AS
SELECT SALES_AREA, CUSTOMER_NAME
FROM SALES_FORCE
WHERE SALES_AREA = 'London'
```

This view defines limited access for users on all customers in the London sales area. The view becomes a table in itself, and remains unaffected by changes in the underlying *Salesforce* table.

## Future trends

Relational database systems seem to be the bedrock of much future computing activity. For instance, RDBMSs are seen by many to be the logical first step in building distributed database systems and knowledge based systems.

A distributed database might be defined as the union of a set of databases held at different locations. RDBMSs are considered to be of primary importance in this area, because of their ability to handle data fragmentation – that is, the ability of a DBMS transparently to combine sets of information held at various remote sites into a coherent single picture for the end-user. This is possible in an RDBMS because of its underlying simple unitary data structure. In a traditional CODASYL-type database the problems of unifying a multitude of complex data structures makes distribution a much more difficult task (Date, 1986).

Many existing RDBMS products benefit from the use of artificial intelligence techniques in such areas as query optimisation, memory management and natural language interfaces. Given that the relational approach has a sound theoretical basis in predicate logic, however, natural connections have been made with the whole area of logic programming and knowledge based systems (KBS). Hence, such initiatives as Japan's fifth generation project in which a RDBMS is intended to form a central core (Feigenbaum and McCorduck, 1984).

## Conclusion

This chapter has discussed some of the key concepts used in defining what is meant by the relational approach to database systems. This approach is undoubtedly here to stay if only because it is an elegant solution to the problem of handling data, and elegant solutions tend to win through.

Probably because of its logical simplicity, the relational model has stimulated a whole range of database design techniques. Perhaps the two most prominent are Codd's notion of normalisation (Codd, 1970), and Chen's notion of entity – relationship (E–R) diagramming (Chen, 1976). These are the topics of the next two chapters.

# 4 Normalisation

## Introduction

In his seminal paper on the relational database model, Codd (1970), formulated a number of good design principles for a relational database. These principles were formalised in terms of three normal forms: first normal form (1NF), second normal form (2NF) and third normal form (3NF). The process of transforming a database through these three normal forms is known as the process of normalisation. Later, 3NF was shown to have certain inadequacies and a stronger form was introduced called the Boyce–Codd form (BCNF) (Codd, 1974). Subsequently Fagin introduced fourth normal form (4NF) and indeed fifth normal form (5NF) (Fagin, 1977, 1979). In this chapter we shall however limit ourselves to discussing BCNF.

Normalisation, then, is a step-by-step technique for transforming data subject to a whole range of file maintenance problems into an organised database free from such problems.

Normalisation can be done in one of two ways. First, by using an informal, step-by-step procedure of directing tables through a number of levels of normalisation (Kent, 1983). Second, by following a formal, and probably more systematic process of drawing determinancy diagrams and applying the Boyce–Codd rule (Howe, 1983).

The first method is the conventional one used in discussing normalisation. We therefore cover this approach first. This will then act as a useful basis for discussing the whole question of determinancy diagrams and the application of the Boyce–Codd rule.

## Advantages of normalisation

1. Eliminating redundancy. A major advantage of the database approach discussed in a previous chapter is that inconsistency is reduced by eliminating redundant data. Care must be taken however to distinguish between duplicated and redundant data. Duplicated data are present when a column of a table has two or more identical values. In contrast,

data are redundant if they can be deleted without information being lost. Redundancy is thus unnecessary duplication. A fully normalised database is one in which such unnecessary duplication is reduced to a minimum.

2. A simpler or more natural data model. Transforming data from an unnormalised to a fully normalised state usually means that the database more clearly reflects the natural entities and relationships in the 'real world'.

3. Avoidance of amendment side-effects. In the table in figure 4.1 there are a number of redundant values in, for instance, the product price attribute. Suppose we now want to change the price of a widget to £1.50. Clearly it is not sufficient to update the first order record for a widget. We have consistently to update all records referring to a widget.

4. Avoidance of deletion side-effects. We meet a similar problem if we wish to delete information from the table in figure 4.1 Suppose we wish to delete order number 1385 from the table. If we did this all information on woggles would be erased from our system. This is clearly inadequate.

5. Avoidance of insertion side-effects. This is the converse of a deletion side-effect. Suppose we wanted to add details of a new customer to our database. Clearly we cannot do this in the present system until such a customer has placed a concrete order with our firm.

```
Order
-----
```

| Order Number | Order Date | Customer Number | Customer Name | Product Number | Product Name | Quantity Ordered | Product Price |
|---|---|---|---|---|---|---|---|
| 1234 | 01/02/88 | 2235 | Jenkins | 4875 | Widget | 200 | 1.00 |
| 1385 | 08/02/88 | 3444 | Jones | 2890 | Woggle | 300 | 2.00 |
| 1567 | 15/02/88 | 3444 | Jones | 4875 | Widget | 1000 | 1.00 |
| 1789 | 21/02/88 | 2980 | Davies | 3332 | Wangle | 150 | 0.50 |
| 2045 | 28/02/88 | 2235 | Jenkins | 3332 | Wangle | 40 | 0.50 |
| 2344 | 01/03/88 | 2235 | Jenkins | 4875 | Widget | 400 | 1.00 |
| 1385 | 08/02/88 | 3444 | Jones | 4875 | Widget | 300 | 1.00 |

*Figure 4.1 Unnormalised table*

**Stages of normalisation**

Normalisation by the informal approach is carried out in four steps:

1. Represent the data as an unnormalised table or relation
2. Transform the unnormalised table to first normal form
3. Transform first normal form tables to second normal form
4. Transform second normal form tables to third normal form

**Representing the data as an unnormalised table**

Suppose we extract the following data items from our analysis of an order form used in the Widget, Woggle and Wangle Company:

```
CUSTOMER NUMBER
CUSTOMER NAME
PRODUCT NUMBER
PRODUCT NAME
QUANTITY ORDERED
PRODUCT PRICE
ORDER NUMBER
ORDER DATE
```

To satisfy the constraints of a relation, as discussed in chapter 3, we have to choose a key for this data set. A key is a data item which satisfies the two characteristics discussed in chapter 2 – a data item whose values are unique and not null. We choose order number to be the primary key for this table, as this is the data item which most clearly satisfies these criteria.

**Unnormalised data to first normal form**

We reduce unnormalised data to first normal form by removing repeating groups and turning such groups into separate relations.

Having chosen a key for the unnormalised relation we then look for a group of attributes or a single attribute that has multiple values for a single value of the key. If such attributes are found, we split them off into a separate relation giving them an appropriate key.

Figure 4.1 represents an unnormalised table containing data to be used by an order processing system. For each order in the system there may be a number of products referred to by the order. This means that the product number, product name, quantity ordered and product price are all likely to repeat in our unnormalised table. We therefore split this information off into its own table, making sure that we maintain the relationship between the information in the two tables through the common attribute order number (figure 4.2).

```
Order
-----

Order    Order     Customer  Customer
Number   Date      Number    Name
------

1234     01/02/88  2235      Jenkins
1385     08/02/88  3444      Jones
1567     15/02/88  3444      Jones
1789     21/02/88  2980      Davies
2045     28/02/88  2235      Jenkins
2344     01/03/88  2235      Jenkins


Order-product
-------------

Order    Product   Product   Quantity  Product
Number   Number    Name      Ordered   Price
------   -------

1234     4875      Widget     200      1.00
1385     2890      Woggle     300      2.00
1567     4875      Widget    1000      1.00
1789     3332      Wangle     150      0.50
2045     3332      Wangle      40      0.50
2344     4875      Widget     400      1.00
1385     4875      Widget     300      1.00
```

*Figure 4.2 First normal form tables (1NF)*

**First normal form to second normal form**

To move from first normal form to second normal form we remove part-key dependencies. This involves examining those relations that have a compound-key (a key made up of two or more attributes) and for each field or attribute asking the question:

Can the field be uniquely identified by part of the compound key, or is the whole of the compound key necessary?

If an attribute or group of attributes can be identified solely through part of the compound key then we form a separate relation.

In our 1NF database in figure 4.2 we have only one table with a compound key – the ORDER-PRODUCT table. For each attribute in this table we ask the questions above. We find that, for the attributes quantity-ordered and product-price, we need both elements of the compound key to identify such items. Product-name and product-price however bear no direct relationship with the order-number; the product-number is sufficient uniquely to identify a product's name and price. We therefore split this information off into its own table.

**Second normal form to third normal form**

We move from second normal form to third normal form by removing inter-data and inter-key dependencies. To do this we examine every relation and ask of each pair of fields in that relation:

Is the value of field A dependent upon the value of field B, or vice versa?

Or, to rephrase the question,

Given a value for field A do we then have only one value for field B?

If the answer to both questions is no, we split off the relevant fields into their own separate relations.

Performing this analysis on the 2NF database in figure 4.3, we should see that in our ORDER table there is a definite inter-data dependency between customer-number and customer-name. In other words, customer-number can be used as an alternative key for the attribute customer-name. In a fully normalised relation, all dependencies must be solely between the key of the table and the attributes of the table. No part-key dependencies are allowed. We therefore split off the customer information into its own table as in figure 4.4.

```
Order
-----

Order    Order      Customer  Customer
Number   Date       Number    Name
------

1234     01/02/88   2235      Jenkins
1385     08/02/88   3444      Jones
1567     15/02/88   3444      Jones
1789     21/02/88   2980      Davies
2045     28/02/88   2235      Jenkins
2344     01/03/88   2235      Jenkins


Order-product
-------------

Order    Product   Quantity
Number   Number    Ordered
------   -------

1234     4875        200
1385     2890        300
1567     4875       1000
1789     3332        150
2045     3332         40
2344     4875        400
1385     4875        300


Product
-------
Product  Product   Product
No       Name      Price
-------

4875     Widget     1.00
2890     Woggle     2.00
3332     Wangle     0.50
```

*Figure 4.3 Second normal form tables (2NF)*

```
Order
-----
Order     Order       Customer
Number    Date        No.
------
1234      01/02/88    2235
1385      08/02/88    3444
1567      15/02/88    3444
1789      21/02/88    2980
2045      28/02/88    2235
2344      01/03/88    2235
```

```
Customer

Customer    Customer
Number      Name
--------
2235        Jenkins
3444        Jones
2980        Davies
```

```
Order-product

Order     Product    Quantity
Number    Number     Ordered
------    -------
1234      4875        200
1385      2890        300
1567      4875       1000
1789      3332        150
2045      3332         40
2344      4875        400
1385      4875        300
```

```
Product
-------
Product   Product    Product
No        Name       Price
-------
4875      Widget      1.00
2890      Woggle      2.00
3332      Wangle      0.50
```

*Figure 4.4 Third normal form tables (3NF)*

**The Boyce–Codd Rule**

A simplification of the Boyce–Codd rule states that:

Every determinant must be the primary key of a table.

We know what a primary key is, it remains to explain what a determinant is. Determinancy, or its reverse, dependency, concerns the association between attributes in a table. If we say that attribute A determines attribute B, we mean that for every instance of A in the table we can visualise one unambiguous value for B.

Hence, in our order processing example above, we can say that customer-number determines customer-name, because if we know a value for the customer-number we can unambiguously locate a corresponding value for customer-name in the table.

Normalisation by the informal approach involves three transformations of a data set:

- remove repeating groups
- remove part-key dependencies
- remove inter-data and inter-key dependencies

Each of these transformations, or rules, involves the consideration of determinancy or dependency.

We now consider a more systematic approach to normalisation based around the application of one rule, the Boyce–Codd rule, to a diagrammatic representation of the determinancy in a table.

**Determinancy diagrams**

It is useful to diagram the determinancy present in some data-set as a first step in generating a normalised set of tables. Such a diagram is said to be a determinancy diagram. In a determinancy diagram, attributes are represented by boxes labelled with the names of the attributes. Determinancy is indicated between attributes by drawing a directed arrow from the determinant attribute (that which is doing the determining) to the dependent attribute (that which is dependent on the other attribute). Hence we draw an arrow from a box containing the attribute customer number to a box containing customer name.

Whenever a compound determinant emerges in our data-set, we draw a box around all of the attributes making up the determinant. The arrow is then drawn from the encompassing box to the dependent attribute.

Occasionally, an example of transitive determinancy emerges. Transitive determinancy involves the situation in which A is said to determine B, and

B is said to determine C. In all such situations, A can hence be said to determine C. One of the major advantages of determinancy diagrams is that such relationships are made more explicit.

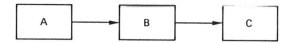

## Applying the Boyce–Codd Rule

Once we have drawn a comprehensive determinancy diagram for our dataset, we then apply the Boyce–Codd rule. This means that for every determinant in our diagram we form a separate table, making the determinant the primary key of the table. All attributes dependent on this determinant are then placed in the table. If however some of these dependent attributes are themselves determinants, we cannot include them in the table (see transitive determinancy above). We must split off such determinants, and their dependent attributes, into their own individual tables.

## Case study: Cindy Cinemas

Suppose our task is to arrive at a fully normalised database for the data needed by the Cindy Cinemas chain as represented in the unnormalised table in figure 4.5.

Cinema

| Film no | Film name | Cinema code | Cinema name | Town | Population | Manager no | Manager name | Takings (£) |
|---------|-----------|-------------|-------------|------|-----------|------------|--------------|-------------|
| 25 | Star Wars | BX | Rex | Cardiff | 300,000 | 01 | Jones | 900 |
| 25 | Star Wars | KT | Rialto | Swansea | 200,000 | 03 | Thomas | 350 |
| 25 | Star Wars | DJ | Odeon | Newport | 250,000 | 01 | Jones | 800 |
| 50 | Jaws | BX | Rex | Cardiff | 300,000 | 01 | Jones | 1,200 |
| 50 | Jaws | DJ | Odeon | Newport | 250,000 | 01 | Jones | 400 |
| 50 | Jaws | TL | Classic | Bridgend | 150,000 | 02 | Davies | 300 |
| 50 | Jaws | RP | Grand | Bristol | 350,000 | 04 | Smith | 1,500 |
| 50 | Jaws | HF | State | Bristol | 350,000 | 04 | Smith | 1,000 |
| 30 | Star Trek | BX | Rex | Cardiff | 300,000 | 01 | Jones | 850 |
| 30 | Star Trek | TL | Classic | Bridgend | 150,000 | 02 | Davies | 500 |
| 40 | ET | KT | Rialto | Swansea | 200,000 | 03 | Davies | 1,200 |
| 40 | ET | RP | Grand | Bristol | 350,000 | 04 | Smith | 2,000 |

*Figure 4.5 Cindy Cinemas*

We draw a determinancy diagram representing this information as in figures 4.6 and 4.7. Note that we need both the film-no and cinema-code to determine takings. We therefore draw an encompassing box around these determinants, and draw an arrow from this box to the takings attribute. Note also the transitive determinancy between cinema-code, town and population, and cinema-code, manager-no and manager-name.

Assuming that we have drawn our diagram correctly, it is now a relatively simple task to transform the determinancy diagram into a set of fully normalised tables as below:

```
TOWN (Town, Population)
      ----
MANAGER (Manager-no, Manager-name)
         ----------
CINEMA (Cinema-code, Cinema-name, Town, Manager)
        -----------
FILM (Film-no, Film-name)
      -------
VENUE (Cinema-code, Film-no, Takings)
       -----------  -------
```

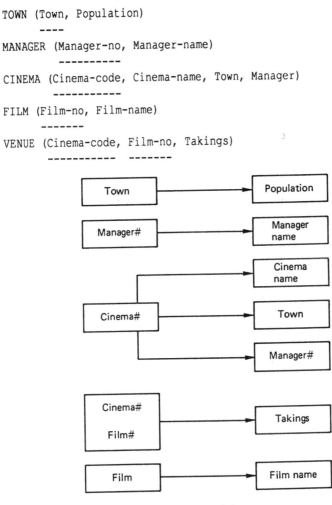

*Figure 4.6*

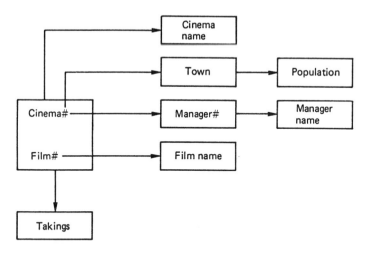

*Figure 4.7*

## Conclusion

Normalisation can be represented by a distortion of the legal 'oath':

1. NO REPEATING
2. THE FIELDS DEPEND UPON THE KEY
3. THE WHOLE KEY
4. AND NOTHING BUT THE KEYS
5. SO HELP ME CODD

Line 5 indicates that the techniques were developed by E.F. Codd in the early 1970s. Line 2 states that all fields in a table must depend upon the key. Given the value of the key field you should be able to determine the value of the other fields in the table. Line 1 indicates that there should be no repeating groups of data in a fully normalised table. Line 3 indicates that tabular fields should depend on the whole of the tables' key, and not just part of it, if it is compound. Finally, line 4 indicates that there should be no inter-data dependencies between fields in a table. The only dependency should be between the key field and all other fields.

There are a number of advantages involved in using normalisation as a database design technique:

1. It operates at the logical level, postponing physical considerations till the latest possible date.
2. It uses some well-defined rules which are relatively straightforward to apply.
3. It uses tangible inputs, rather than conceptual views of data, eg., input documents, existing files, or planned output.
4. It provides a foundation for defining and structuring a systems data such that it will not be subject to file maintenance problems.

Having said this, very few analysts would treat the organisation proposed by 3NF relations as gospel, if only because in any real-life situation normalisation would probably propose too many files to be practically manageable. Some sites may therefore regard 1NF as being good enough for them if the data volumes are small. Other sites may consider 2NF relations to be sufficiently flexible to meet their needs at higher volumes of data. Yet other sites may merge bits of 3NF relations together to optimise processing requirements (figure 4.8).

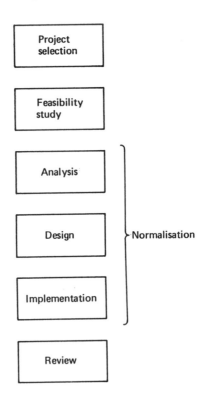

*Figure 4.8*

**Problems**

1. Define the term normalisation.
2. What are deletion, insertion and amendment side-effects?
3. What is removed from a relation when it is converted to first normal form (1NF)?
4. What is removed from a relation when it is converted to second normal form (2NF)?
5. What is removed from a relation when it is converted to third normal form (3NF)?
6. List some of the advantages of using a formal rather than an informal approach to normalisation.
7. Generate a fully normalised set of tables from the following un-normalised table.

```
Operating Schedule
------------------
```

| Doctor No. | Doctor Name | Operation No. | Operation Date | Operation Time | Patient No. | Patient Name | Date Of Admission |
|---|---|---|---|---|---|---|---|
| 18654 | Smith | AA1234 | 04/02/88 | 08:30 | 2468 | M.Davies | 20/01/88 |
| 18654 | Smith | BA1598 | 04/02/88 | 10:30 | 3542 | D.Jones | 11/01/88 |
| 18654 | Smith | FG1965 | 04/02/88 | 16:00 | 1287 | I.Evans | 25/12/87 |
| 18654 | Smith | AA1235 | 13/02/88 | 08:30 | 2468 | M.Davies | 20/01/88 |
| 13855 | Evans | LP1564 | 13/02/88 | 14:00 | 4443 | P.Beynon | 05/01/88 |
| 18592 | Jones | PP9900 | 15/02/88 | 14:00 | 2222 | I.Scott | 04/01/88 |
| 18592 | Jones | BA1598 | 04/02/88 | 10:30 | 3542 | D.Jones | 11/01/88 |
| 18592 | Jones | FG1965 | 04/02/88 | 16:00 | 1287 | I.Evans | 25/12/87 |

8. Draw a determinancy diagram for the set of tables in figure 4.4.

# 5 Entity–relationship Diagramming

## Introduction

Entity–relationship diagramming (E–R diagramming) is not a new concept. In fact, this type of modelling is probably one of the oldest techniques associated with database design. Although the technique of E–R diagramming is now usually equated with the relational database model, it had its beginnings in theoretical work conducted on the hierarchical and network models by Charles Bachmann and the CODASYL Data Base Task Group (Bachmann, 1969; CODASYL 1971). Probably the most influential paper on database design was, however, one which attempted to integrate much of the earlier material on the subject (Chen, 1976). It is Chen's paper which established the technique and the notation that we shall be discussing in this chapter.

Basically, an E–R diagram is what it says. It is a model of an information system in terms of entities and the relationships between entities. The assumption underlying the technique is that there is a 'real world' which can be modelled in terms of entities and relationships (Klein and Hirschheim, 1987). This we might refer to as an *entity model*. An E–R diagram is a method for representing such an entity model in pictorial form.

## Entities and entity types

An entity may be defined as:

> a thing which the enterprise recognises as being capable of an independent existence and which can be uniquely identified (Howe, 1983).

The two most important facets of this definition are:

- Independent existence
- Unique identification

An entity may be an object such as a house or a car or an event such as a house sale or a car service. In information terms the characteristics of independent existence and unique identification normally define what we

38

might call a *data group*; that is, a group of data items or attributes associated with a particular entity.

Imagine, for instance, a basic personnel system. Typically there might be a number of entities in this environment which we could readily define:

- person
- department
- grade
- position

Each of these entities could be described by a group of attributes as follows:

| Person | Department | Grade | Position |
|--------|-----------|-------|----------|
| Personnel No. | Dept. No. | Grade Code | Position Code |
| Name | Dept. Name | Grade Desc. | Description |
| Address | Establishment No. | Days Vacation | Dept. No. |
| Grade Code | Location | Company Car | Min. Yrs Serv. |
| No. of Years | Manager's Name | Value  Min. | Educ Level |
| Service | | Profit Share | |
| Dept. No. | | | Scheme No. |
| Date of Birth | | | |
| Date Joined | | | |

A distinction is often drawn between an entity type and an entity. The name of an entity together with its attributes define an entity type of which there may be many instances. An instance of an entity type, which is an entity, is an occurrence of that type for which actual values of the attributes have been given. So long as we are aware of this distinction it is usually safe to use the terms entity and entity type almost synonymously, as we shall do in the following discussion.

## Relationship

A relationship can be defined as:

an association between two or more entities (Howe, 1983).

In terms of the data groups describing two entities, a relationship can be said to exist if an attribute is common to both data groups. For example, a relationship exists between Grade and Person in the personnel system described above through the attribute Grade Code which is common to both data groups.

More than one relationship can exist between any two entities. For example, the entities House and Person can be related by ownership and/or by occupation. In theory, having identified a set of $N$ entities, up to $1/2\ N(N - 1)$ relationships could exist between these entities. In practice, it will usually be obvious that many entities are quite unrelated. Furthermore, the object of the technique is to document only so-called direct relationships. For instance, direct relationships exist between the entities Parent and Child, and between Child and School, but the relationship between Parent and School is indirect; it exists only by virtue of the Child entity (Shave, 1981).

### Entity, attribute and relationship definitions re-examined

The objects needed to support a given information system do not usually fall irrevocably into one of the three categories entity, attribute or relationship. A classic example is provided by data on marriages (Chen, 1976). The object marriage could be regarded as an entity with attributes such as date, place and name of the bride and groom. It could similarly be regarded as an attribute, that is, as a status associated with the entity Person. Finally, it could be regarded as a relationship, perhaps connecting the entities Man and Woman.

One of the tasks of the E–R diagrammer is to decide which of these viewpoints is the most appropriate for the system under consideration. Hence, data analysis of this form is often referred to as *semantic modelling* (Date, 1986). In other words, the aim is to describe the items and relationships of data as they are perceived in the organisation involved, not as they have to be in order to conform to the rules of a particular system of implementation (Klein and Hirschheim, 1987).

### Notation

The end-product of E–R diagramming is a model of the entities and relationships in a particular application environment.

We indicate an entity on the model by a rectangular box in which is written a meaningful name for the entity. For example:

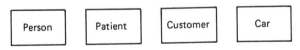

We indicate a relationship between two entities by drawing a labelled line between the relevant boxes on our entity model, for example:

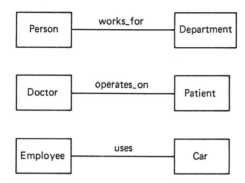

## The degree of a relationship

There are a number of properties of the concept of a relationship that are usually considered important. The most important of which is the degree of a relationship. A relationship can be said to be either a 1:1 (one-to-one) relationship, a 1:*M* (one-to-many) relationship, or a *M:N* (many-to-many) relationship.

For instance, the relationship between salesmen and customers can be said to be one-to-one (1:1) if it can be defined in the following way:

• A salesman services at most one customer.
• A customer is serviced by at most one salesman.

In contrast, the relationship between salesmen and customers is one-to-many (1:*M*) if it is defined as:

• A salesman services many customers.
• A customer may be serviced by at most one salesman.

Finally, we are approaching a realistic representation of the relationship when we describe it as being many-to-many (*M:N*):

• A salesman services many customers.
• A customer may be serviced by many salesmen.

There are a number of competing notational devices available for portraying the degree of a relationship. We choose to represent degree by drawing a crow's foot on the 'many' end of a relationship. The crow's foot is chosen because:

• It provides some intuitive feel for there being many instances of an entity.
• It does not readily confuse with an arrowhead, as used in a data-flow diagram to indicate data flow.

Many people maintain that crow's feet should only be drawn down the page. They refer to a crow's foot that is drawn up the page as a 'dead crow', and to a Crow's foot that appears across the page as a 'sick crow'.

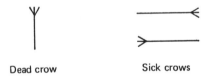

Dead crow         Sick crows

The author is unconvinced by these metaphors; hence the diagrams in this book will contain many dead and sick crows.

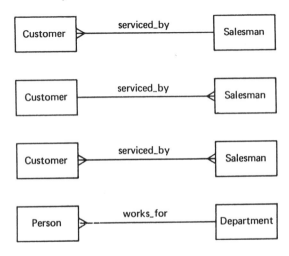

### Membership class

Another important property of a relationship concerns the participation of each entity in the relationship. For some entity we might say that every occurrence of that entity participates in the relationship. For other entities it may be true to say that occurrences of the entity can exist independently.

For example, suppose that the relationship employed between an employee and a department can be detailed as follows:

- Every employee must be employed within a department.
- A department may exist without any employees.

For this relationship we say that membership of employee in the 'employs' relationship is mandatory, in other words an employee occurrence must participate in the 'employs' relationship. In contrast, the membership of department in the 'employs' relationship is optional; in other words, a department occurrence can exist without participating in the 'employs' relationship.

Knowledge of the membership classes of entities is important, as it may influence the design of a particular database.

## Notation

When an entity's membership class is mandatory, we draw a dot inside the entity symbol. When it is optional we draw the dot on the relationship line, prior to any crow's foot.

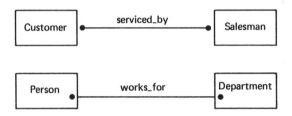

## Validating an E–R diagram against requirements

A first-pass E–R diagram represents the basic structure of objects needed in a given information system. Most of the adherents of the technique recommend that this model should be validated against some definition of system requirements. This definition will identify which entities and relationships must be accessed, in what order, by what means, and for what purpose.

For instance, suppose we have the following extract from an E–R diagram which represents the relationships between entities in an educational setting (Shave, 1981):

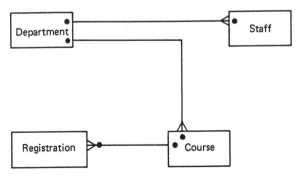

We wish to validate this extract against a system requirement to determine the staff/student ratio for a given department. To perform this analysis we need to access:

- All staff of a department
- Each course taught by a member of staff
- Each member of staff associated with a course
- Each registration of a student for a course in a department.

This we can do with our E–R diagram, as indicated by the arrows:

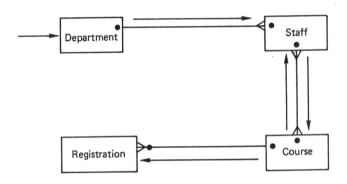

### Top-down v. bottom-up data modelling

Normalisation as described in the previous chapter is a bottom-up data modelling procedure. It involves the following stages:

- Select the attributes of interest.
- Combine these attributes into fully-normalised tables.

Although this bottom-up procedure works relatively well in simple situations, it does suffer from problems when applied to more realistic situations where there may be a large number of attributes to consider or a large number of relationships between entities.

These problems can be overcome by using a top-down approach in which the sequence of operations is:

- Select the entities and relationships of interest to the organisation.
- Assign attributes and relationships to these entities in such a way that a set of fully normalised tables is obtained (Gillenson, 1987).

In the remaining sections of this chapter we shall consider E–R diagramming as a top-down data analysis technique in more detail. In particular, we will consider how it is possible to exploit a number of straightforward rules for moving from an entity model to a set of tables.

**Assignment rules**

Once we have drawn our entity relationship diagram we then apply a number of straightforward rules for attribute assignment to each entity to entity relationship on our diagram.

*1:1 relationship*

Let us suppose we wish to assign company cars to employees on a one-to-one basis. In terms of a 1:1 relationship, the relevant table structures will be determined purely on the basis of the membership class of the entities.

- Membership mandatory for both entity types. *Put all the attributes in a single table:*

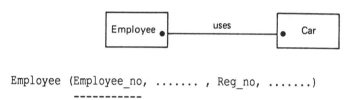

```
Employee (Employee_no, ....... , Reg_no, .......)
          -----------
```

Since we have no null values for employee information or car information, we can bundle all the data in one table.
- *Membership mandatory for only one entity type.* Generate two tables and post the identifier of the mandatory table into the optional table:

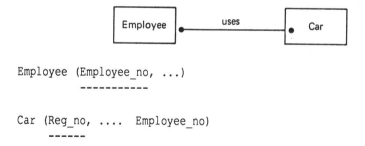

```
Employee (Employee_no, ...)
          -----------

Car (Reg_no, ....  Employee_no)
     ------
```

It is now possible for there to exist company employees who do not use company cars. Bundling all the information in one table is therefore no longer feasible, since the car information is optional (potentially null) for certain employees.
- *Membership optional for both entity types.* Have three tables, one for each entity and one for the relationship:

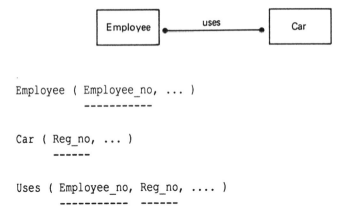

```
Employee ( Employee_no, ... )
           ----------

Car ( Reg_no, ... )
      ------

Uses ( Employee_no, Reg_no, .... )
       ----------  ------
```

We now have a situation in which employees do not necessarily have company cars, and cars, perhaps those newly acquired, are not necessarily used by company employees. Since both the employees information, and car information is now optional, we fragment the structure into three tables: one table for each entity, and one table for the relationship.

### 1:M Relationship

Let us now use another example to illustrate the transformation process appropriate for a one-to-many relationship. Here we have a situation in which a given hospital ward contains many patients.

- *Membership of 'many' entity is mandatory.* Create two tables and post the identifier of the 'one' table into the 'many' table:

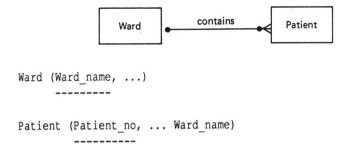

```
Ward (Ward_name, ...)
      ---------

Patient (Patient_no, ... Ward_name)
         ----------
```

- *Membership of 'many' entity is optional.* Create three tables, one for each entity and one for the relationship:

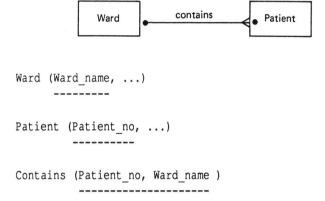

```
Ward (Ward_name, ...)
      ---------

Patient (Patient_no, ...)
         ----------

Contains (Patient_no, Ward_name )
          ----------------------
```

In the case of a one-to-many relationship, we must always have at least two tables. If we tried, for instance, to represent ward and patient information in one table, the ward information would repeat. If the patient entity is also optional, we need an additional table to prevent null instances of patient information from occurring.

### M:N Relationship

In all cases create three tables, one for each entity and one for the relationship:

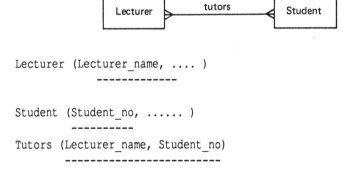

```
Lecturer (Lecturer_name, .... )
          -------------

Student (Student_no, ...... )
         ----------
Tutors (Lecturer_name, Student_no)
        --------------------------
```

In the case of a many-to-many relationship, the membership class of the entities is unimportant.

**Conclusion**

To summarise, E–R diagramming involves the following steps:

- Identify an initial set of entities from the environment.
- Investigate and record inter-relationships.
- Draw a diagram to represent entities and relationships.
- Indicate the degree and membership class of each of the relationships on the diagram.
- Validate the structure against the system requirements.
- Rationalise the structure.
- Revalidate.
- Convert the diagram into a set of fully normalised tables.

E–R diagramming is primarily a database design technique. An E–R diagram comprises a conceptual model of the system database. From this model we can derive a set of logical record or table structures, which represent the database in normalised form. The final step is to convert these logical record structures into physical record structures. This is often referred to as 'flexing' the model, and involves at least two procedures. First, we validate the model against requirements. This will often mean that we incorporate extra bits into our model or perhaps move back from a fully normalised form to satisfy access or storage requirements. Second, we convert the logical table structures into a form appropriate for the particular DBMS. If the DBMS is of the relational kind the transformation is relatively straightforward. If the DBMS is hierarchical or network, the process is a little more convoluted but not difficult. For those interested in a discussion of such issues see (Howe, 1983) (See also figure 5.1.)

**Case study: a general hospital appointments and operations system**

Let us suppose that we are given the brief of designing an appropriate information system for the patients' appointments and operations activities of a large general hospital. Our initial analysis provides us with the following brief description of the existing manual system.

- Patients are dealt with by an appointment system.
- Patients must make an appointment for a clinic session held at one of the hospital's clinics.
- Doctors are allocated one or more appointments within a clinic session, but only one doctor will be present at each appointment.
- Operations are scheduled and allocated to one of a number of theatre sessions held in the hospital's operating theatres. Each doctor may perform a number of given operations on patients.

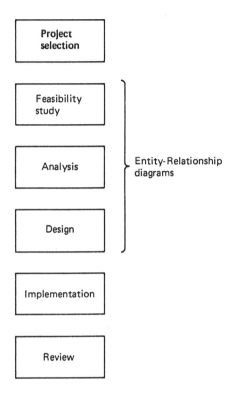

*Figure 5.1*

From such a description, we can get some initial idea of the important entities in our system. These are:

```
HOSPITAL
CLINIC
CLINIC-SESSION
APPOINTMENT
PATIENT
DOCTOR
OPERATION
OPERATING-THEATRE
THEATRE-SESSION
```

The text also gives us some notion of the relationships involved between these entities. We document these on a grid as follows, where a cross in the appropriate cell on the grid indicates a relationship between two entities:

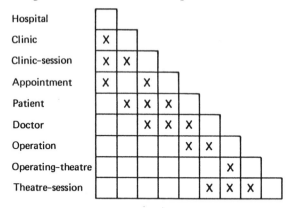

It is a comparatively straightforward process to convert the information on this grid into a 'first-pass' E–R diagram. This gives a diagram of boxes and lines as in figure 5.2.

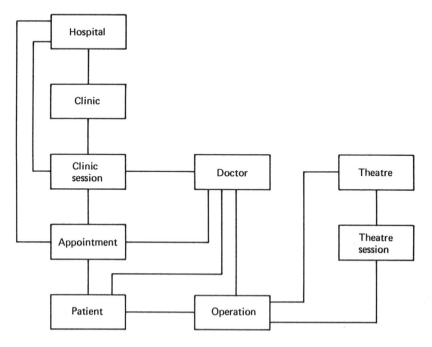

*Figure 5.2*

Once we have drawn boxes to represent the entities and lines to indicate the relationships, we can then attempt to investigate the degree of each of the relationships on the diagram. For instance, it is clear from the text that there is only one hospital, which has many clinics. We indicate this on the diagram by drawing a crow's foot on the clinic end of the hospital–clinic line.

For some of the other relationships on the diagram we need further information. This highlights the important role that E–R diagramming has as a systems analysis tool. In other words, it is an excellent vehicle for highlighting areas or topics for further investigation.

Suppose that our further investigations lead us to conclude the following facts. Each clinic holds a number of clinic sessions, but any one clinic session is held at only one clinic. Likewise, a clinic session is made up of a number of appointments, but an appointment is made with only one clinic session. These facts can now be incorporated into our diagram (figure 5.3 ).

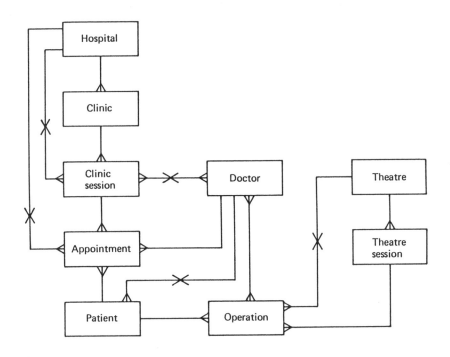

*Figure 5.3*

We now attempt to rationalise the diagram. Rationalisation is the process of identifying and removing redundant relationships, that is, those links that are unnecessary to fulfil the 'natural' data relationships in the system. What we are trying to achieve initially is a model which minimally represents the system under investigation. In practice of course, we would usually have to revise this minimal model in order to reflect the storage and access requirements of the information system. This would usually mean adding extra entities and relationships to improve performance. The redundant relationships in the present model have been indicated on figure 5.3 by lines marked with a cross.

The final step on the way to arriving at a set of tables for the appointments and operations system is to attempt to assign an appropriate membership class to each of the relationships on the diagram. A possible assignment might be as shown in figure 5.4.

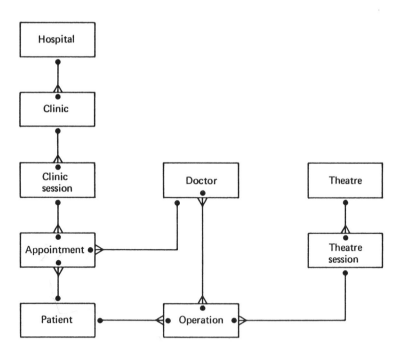

*Figure 5.4*

From the final E–R diagram we construct a set of fully normalised tables as follows:

HOSPITAL (Hospital_name, ...)
         -------------

CLINIC (Clinic_name, Hospital_name, ...)
       -----------

CLINIC_SESSION (Clinic_name, Session_no, ...)
               ----------- ----------

APPOINTMENT (Clinic_name, Session_no, Patient_no, Doctor_no, ...)
            ----------- ----------- ----------

PATIENT (Patient_no, ...)
        ----------

DOCTOR (Doctor_no, ...)
       ---------

OPERATION (Operation_no, Theatre_name, Theatre_session, Patient_no...)
          ------------ ------------- ---------------

DOCTOR_OPERATION_SCHEDULE (Doctor_no, Operation_no, ...)
                          ----------- -------------

THEATRE (Theatre_name, ...)
        ------------

THEATRE_SESSION (Theatre_name, Theatre_session, ...)
                ------------ ---------------

## Problems

1. What are the other relationships in the personnel database described on page 39.
2. Using some sensible assumptions about the degree of and membership class of each of the relationships, draw an entity–relationship diagram to represent the entities and relationship in the personnel database.

3. Without having a set of requirements with which to validate the structure of entities and relationships, there appears to be one redundant relationship on the diagram. Which is it?

4. A subsidiary of the Standard Stationery Company sells office products within South Wales.

   For selling purposes, South Wales is divided up by the subsidiary into four areas. Three of the areas centre around the cities of Newport, Cardiff and Swansea. The other area covers the numerous small townships in the South Wales valleys.

   Four salesmen are appointed to handle these sales areas, which each contain a number of customers of Standard Stationery. Salesmen sell a range of products to customers. Sales are debited from stock held at local warehouses. When stock of a particular product is suitably depleted, a quantity is reordered from the supplier. Standard Stationery maintain a policy of ordering any particular product from only one supplier, although a range of products may be supplied by any one supplier.

   Draw an E–R diagram to represent the situation at Standard Stationery.

# 6  Data-flow Diagramming

## Introduction

A data flow diagram (DFD) is a representation of a system or subsystem in terms of how data or information moves through the system. Data-flow diagramming is therefore a technique for the dynamic modelling of information systems: a process analysis rather than a data analysis technique.

A number of persons have been involved in developing the data-flow diagram as an analysis and design tool. Among the earliest exponents of the method were Tom De-Marco and Edward Yourdon (De-Marco, 1979a,b). Gane and Sarson (1977) have modified and extended the technique to approach something like the technique that we shall be using. The major difference of our technique is in the notation. We shall be using the notation recommended within the British methodology SSADM (Cutts, 1987) (Structured Systems Analysis and Design Methodology: see chapter 15).

## Why use data flow diagrams?

The two main competitors to DFDs in terms of a means for systems analysis and specification are conventional narrative and traditional systems flowcharts. DFDs have a number of advantages over these media (Weinberg, 1980):

1. Conventional Narrative (Underwood, 1984).
   - Two-dimensional inter-connection is more easily shown on a diagram.
   - Descriptive information is included in the symbols of a diagram. This makes diagrams:
   Easier to produce
   Easier to understand
   Much more concise.
   - Rough versions of diagrams are easily made.
   - Data-flow diagrams can be used to show progressive levels of detail.
2. Traditional flowcharting.
   - Data-flow diagrams are simpler than traditional flowcharts. They use fewer symbols.

- They are hence easier to understand by users.
- DFDs are more abstract than system flowcharts. They are less tied to specific implementation details, and are therefore a better means for logical modelling.

### The plumbing analogy

In abstract terms, an information system may be considered as being made up of a number of components:

- Outputs.
- Inputs.
- Processes.
- Stored data.
- People.

Data-flow diagrams attempt to represent at least the first four aspects of an information system.

Probably the easiest way to understand the rationale behind a DFD is to make the analogy between an information system and a household plumbing system. Plumbing systems are designed to handle flows of water; information systems are designed to handle flows of data. A plumbing system receives its water from external sources such as the public water supply, and deposits its used water in external entities such as drains. An information system receives its data from external sources such as customers, banks, retailers, etc., and communicates the results of its processing to other entities, perhaps other information systems. Household plumbing systems are usually designed to process water in some way. For instance, a boiler engages in the process of heating the water to a given temperature. In information systems far more diverse processing occurs: data are transformed by some process and then passed on to another process, and so on. Finally, in a plumbing system there are usually repositories of water, for example, sinks, cisterns etc. In information systems, such repositories are referred to as data stores.

### Elements

A DFD is therefore made up of four basic elements:

- Processes.
- Data Flows.
- Data Stores.
- External Entities.

Let us consider each of these in turn, detailing a brief definition, an appropriate notation, and a set of conventions to guide the newcomer to the technique.

## Process

A process is a transformation of incoming data flow(s) into outgoing data flow(s). For example, verifying the credit status of a customer is a process. A process is represented on a DFD by a labelled square or rectangle. For example:

```
┌─────────────────┐        ┌─────────────────┐
│ Produce customer│        │ Verify customer │
│ invoice         │        │ credit status   │
│                 │        │                 │
└─────────────────┘        └─────────────────┘
```

### *Conventions*

- No two processes should have the same name. This is really to enable processes to form unique elements in a data dictionary (see chapter 7).
- Each process should precisely state a transformation. Labels for processes hence usually include some form of verb: verify, store, record, compute, etc.

## Data flow

A data flow is a pipeline through which packets of information of known composition flow. For example, customer orders, management queries, and sales invoices are all data flows. Data flow is represented on a DFD by a labelled directed arrow. For example:

Customer orders

Sales invoices

Management queries

## Conventions

- A data flow is not a representation of the flow of control:

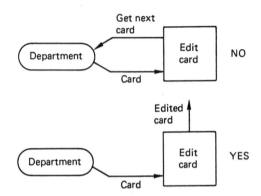

- Every data flow should have an associated meaningful label:

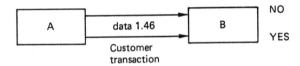

- No two flows should be named the same. Input data to a process should not appear as output from that process. If it does then it has not been transformed.

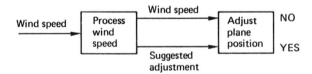

- Do data flows pass through processes to get to another process? If so, redraw that part of the diagram so that data is shown as direct input to the the process that uses it:

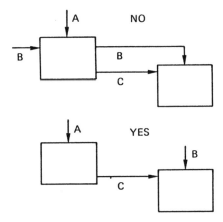

- A process is subject to the 'conservation of data' principle. That is, a process cannot create new data. New data can only come from external entities. A process may only take its input data and transform it in some way to make output data.

## Data store

- A data store is a repository of data. For example, a waste-paper basket, a register, a card index, an indexed-sequential file on tape. A data store is represented on a DFD by an open rectangle or box with an appropriate label. For example:

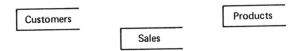

## *Conventions*

A data store can be read, written to, or read and written to:

Data stores are conventionally labelled with plural nouns to emphasise the multiple instances of the information contained within the data store. A consistent naming convention is usually applied to data stores. In other words, it is not considered wise to name a store CUSTOMERS in one place and CUSTOMER DETAILS in another place, if it stores the same information.

- A data store is also subject to the 'conservation of data' principle. That is, that what comes out of a data store must first go in. It is not possible for a data store to create new data out of 'thin air'.

**External entity**

An external entity (also called a source or sink) is something (usually a person, department or organisation), lying outside the context of the system, that is, a net originator or receiver of system data. An external entity is represented on a DFD by some form of rounded shape – a circle, an oval or a lozenge – with an appropriate name. For example:

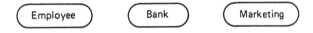

*Conventions*

- The important part of the above definition is 'lying outside the context of the system'. A person, department or organisation lying inside the context of the system would be characterised by the processes they perform. This function portrays entities as means for defining system boundaries.

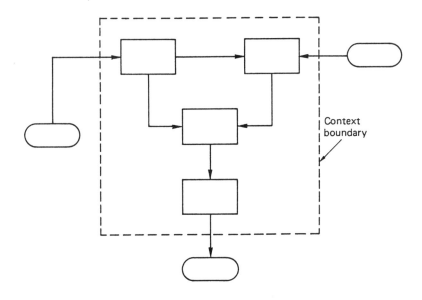

- It is traditional to label external entities with a singular noun. We talk of a bank, not of banks, of an employee, not of employees.

**Additions to the basic notation**

When analysing systems it has been found useful to add the following two constructs to the basic DFD notation:

- Materials or goods flow
- Documents flow.

*Materials or goods flow*

In looking for a place to start, analysts often concentrate initially on the physical things that move through a system. Such items can be drawn on a DFD as a broad labelled arrow. For example:

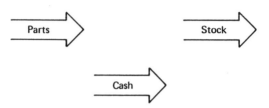

## *Conventions*

It is conventional to draw such materials flow as coming from an entity or process, and going to an entity or process. No connection is made to data stores.

## *Documents flow*

One of the most important requirements of early analysis is to make sure that all relevant documents such as invoices and order forms that apply to a system are collected and examined. It has therefore been found useful to record such documents by name on the DFD. This is done by drawing a traditional document symbol on a data flow. For example:

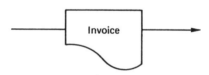

## Levelling or partitioning the problem

All information systems can be characterised by some form of hierarchy. That is, as being made up of a set of processes which are themselves information systems. As a representation of information systems, data-flow diagrams are also characterised by such hierarchical organisation.

Most real-life systems are too involved to represent as a DFD on one single sheet of paper. In representing an information system we therefore have to approach the problem in a top-down manner. We attempt to level the problem beginning with a context diagram of the entire system. As a minimum this might be made up of one process with associated flows, stores and entities. We then take the process or processes represented on the context DFD and break them down into their own DFDs. We continue this decomposition process for a number of levels until we can represent the entire system in sufficient detail (figure 6.1).

A common question asked by newcomers to the DFD technique relates to the number of levels in a DFD hierarchy. How do we know how many levels is sufficient to represent a system satisfactorily? It is impossible to give firm answers to this question. A rough guideline is that an appropriately partitioned system is one in which no individual diagram has more than nine processes represented on it. It is argued that a diagram having fewer than 10 processes does not violate the limitations of human short-term memory (Miller, 1967).

## Heading, balancing and numbering

Given that our system of DFDs represent a hierarchically organised documentation system, a number of conventions are normally applied to the construction of such a system.

First, each DFD should be headed with the name of its parent process. In the case of the overview diagram this will of course constitute the title of the system. For all other DFDs it will refer to the master process which is 'exploded' in the present DFD.

Second, all inputs and outputs between parent and child diagrams should be 'balanced'. This means that, if flows A and B input to process 1 and flow C outputs, then the child diagram should also detail flows A, B and C.

Third, to indicate the position in the DFD hierarchy of any particular process it is useful to number each process uniquely within our documentation system. Such numbering is also useful as a means of referencing a *data dictionary*, to be discussed in chapter 7 (figure 6.1).

## Logical and physical systems

The diagram in figure 6.2 is usually referred to as a model of the current physical system. It is a high-level description of how a valuer presently undertakes the process of property valuation. In contrast, figure 6.3 is a logical model of the activities undertaken by a valuer.

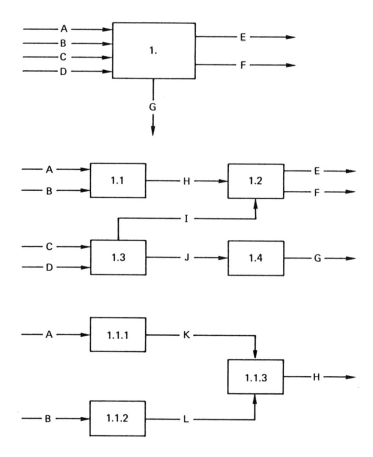

*Figure 6.1*

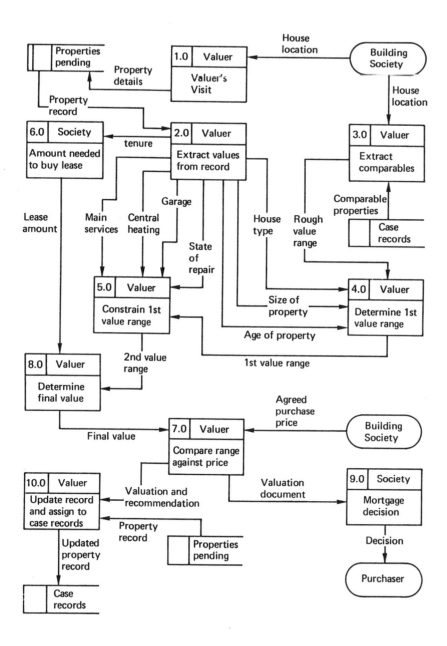

*Figure 6.2*

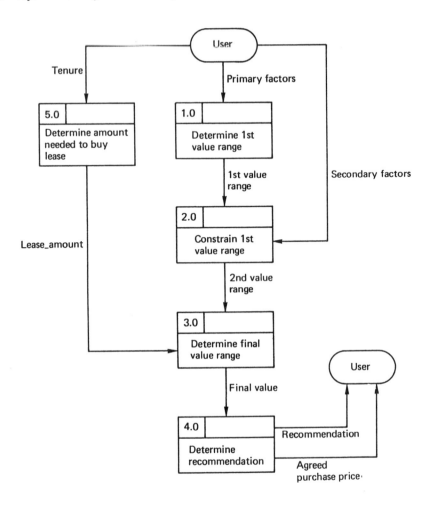

*Figure 6.3*

Logical DFDs tell us what is going on; they do not tell us how the things are done or who does them. Logical DFDs assist analysts in getting a clear picture of what the system is to achieve without concerning themselves too much about implementation details.

It is always easier, however, to start with something concrete. Physical systems can be readily identified and documented. This is why analysts usually start modelling physical systems first, and then attempt to convert physical models into logical models.

In structured systems analysis and design, DFDs are therefore used in at least four different ways, to represent:

- The current physical system.
- The current logical system; that is, the existing system described purely in functional terms.
- The proposed logical system.
- The proposed physical system; that is, a detailed representation of the workings of the proposed system.

Figures 6.2 and 6.3 illustrate the process of transforming a physical DFD into a more abstract functional representation of the problem.

**Constructing a DFD**

Most people introduced to the DFD technique, particularly those with a traditional systems background, find great difficulty in constructing a set of DFDs to represent an information system. This is probably the result of a process-oriented 'mind-set', generated by exposure to third-generation language programming and techniques such as traditional flowcharting.

Data-flow diagramming is fundamentally different from tradtional flowcharting. Flowcharting is a technique for representing process or system logic which is steeped in implementation or physical detail. Data-flow diagramming is a technique for representing the workings of existing information systems or specifying the requirements of new systems in logical terms. Thus, it is largely divorced from implementation details.

As we shall discuss in chapter 13, data-flow diagramming fits in well with notions of specifying a solution to a problem in a declarative rather than a procedural or imperative manner; that is, in terms of 'what' rather than 'how'. As a result of this, some suggested guidelines for constructing a documentation system composed of DFDs are given below.

- Start with a name which adequately describes the information system, for example, VIDEO SHOP SYSTEM.
- Identify the major activities for the information system. For example:

CREATING A MEMBER.
ISSUING A VIDEO.
RETURNING A VIDEO.
RESERVING A VIDEO.
ENQUIRING OF LOANS, VIDEOS, AND/OR MEMBERS.
ACQUIRING NEW VIDEOS.

For each of these major activities, identify the sub-activities that go to make up the process. For example:

CREATING A MEMBER.
  REQUESTING IDENTIFICATION.
  RECORDING MEMBERSHIP DETAILS.
  PRODUCING A MEMBERSHIP CARD.
ISSUING A VIDEO.
  RECORDING HIRE DETAILS.
  RETRIEVING THE VIDEO.
  REQUESTING PAYMENT.
  HANDING OVER THE VIDEO.
RETURNING A VIDEO.
  RECEIVING THE VIDEO.
  CHECKING FOR RESERVED STATUS.
  CHECKING FOR OVERDUE STATUS.
  SCRUBBING HIRE DETAILS.
RESERVING A VIDEO.
  EXTRACTING VIDEO DETAILS.
  MAKING A RESERVATION MARK.
ENQUIRING OF LOANS, VIDEOS, AND/OR MEMBERS.
  IDENTIFYING PURPOSE OF QUERY.
  ANSWERING QUERY.
ACQUIRING NEW VIDEOS.
  ORDERING A NEW VIDEO.
  RECEIVING A NEW VIDEO.

- To draw a context diagram, identify the major external entities that will be used to define the boundaries of the proposed information system, for example, MEMBER, SUPPLIER etc. Place a single process box with a label for the entire system in the centre of the page and arrange the various external entities around it. Then consider the data flows between the external entities and the information system.
- Draw an overview diagram to represent the interaction of the major activities of the system. Represent each major activity as a process box. Transfer the flows on the context diagram on to the overview diagram. Consider the internal flows between processes. Take each of the major activities and draw a data-flow diagram to represent it. Represent each of the sub-activities as a process box. Locate the external entities on the fringes of the page and consider the flows between them and the internal processes. Also ensure that any internal flows on the overview diagram are duly represented on the second-level diagram.
- Iterate up and down between the various levels of DFD. If we add extra process boxes and flows at the lowest level consider how this might affect the higher levels. Likewise, if we make changes to the

context or overview diagram, consider if any changes need to be made to the lower-level diagrams.


### Case study: the Fast Foods system

Fast Foods is a business serving small retailers. Such retailers order canned foods and dry items (sugar, tea, rice) from Fast Foods in bulk quantities such as cases or cartons. Fast Foods holds no stock, but orders in bulk from wholesalers at correspondingly discounted prices. When the bulk supplies arrive, the retailer's orders are filled and despatched.

Before orders are processed, retailers are checked for credit status. If such credit status is unacceptable, the retailer is requested to send cash with order. This usually means that Fast Foods holds the order while the customer is requested for prepayment.

Fast Foods operates a discount policy. Such discounts are determined by the total value of the order and the status of the retailer, particularly whether or not they pay their bills promptly.

Retailers order goods by detailing manufacturer and product name or by specifying a standard product code, which identifies the manufacturer as well as the product. Such information is written on a standard sales order by the retailer and sent to Fast Foods. Fast Foods distributes a catalogue of their products to retailers, together with a set of order forms on a regular basis.

The main documents used in the Fast Foods system are:

1. A sales order from the retailer.
2. A purchase order to the wholesaler.
3. A delivery note from the wholesaler.
4. A shipping note to the retailer.
5. Invoices to the retailer and wholesaler.
6. Remittance advices from the retailer to the wholesaler.

A DFD representing this system is presented in figure 6.4. A number of points should be borne in mind about this diagram. Assumptions have been made in drawing this DFD. These are necessary in the sense that the narrative description detailed above does not provide enough information to produce a sensible solution to the problem. Most of the assumptions made incorporate background knowledge or commonsense reasoning. For instance, there is nothing in the descriptive text to indicate how a purchase order is produced from retailer sales orders. It seems sensible, however, to indicate that some form of batching process occurs. Sales orders are accumulated until a satisfactory sizeable bulk order for a particular product is constructed.

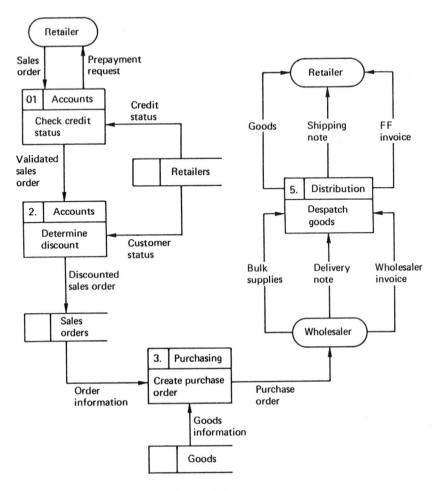

*Figure 6.4*

Drawing a DFD before all the information is known is a perfectly valid exercise. We are using the DFD in this case as an analysis tool. We are making a first attempt at understanding the problem by drawing an initial description. This exercise should highlight many questions which we need to ask our users. We then take this diagram along to our users and use it as a means to extract the further information we need. The diagram is redrawn, taken back to the users, and the whole process repeated until we are happy that our diagrams adequately and accurately specify the workings of the current system.

We say 'diagrams' because the one diagram presented in figure 6.4 is clearly not sufficient to describe the operation of Fast Foods. It is adequate as a first attempt at overview description. Eventually, however, we want to move to a situation where we have specified the system in terms of a hierarchical set of DFDs.

## Conclusion

Data flow diagrams might be summarised as follows:

- They are composed of: processes, flows, entities, stores.
- They are 'levelled'; in that the first DFD represents a general description and subsequent diagrams represent increasing levels of detail.
- They are supported by a data dictionary.

DFDs have been much used in modern systems analysis and design. Indeed, it might be said that most contemporary development methodologies exploit the technique in some form. This probably results from the fact that it is an extremely effective technique applicable in various ways to a number of points in the systems development life-cycle (figure 6.5).

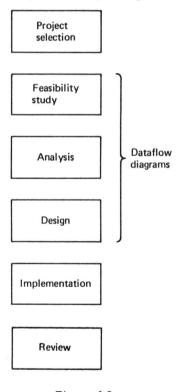

*Figure 6.5*

## Problems

1. How would you defend the statement: 'a major advantage of using DFDs is that they free the systems analyst from a premature commitment to technical implementation details'?

2. What are the main advantages of using a DFD as opposed to a narrative description of some problem?

3. What is wrong with the following DFD extracts?

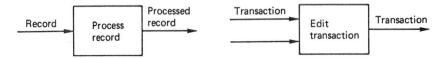

4. What is wrong with the following DFD hierarchy?

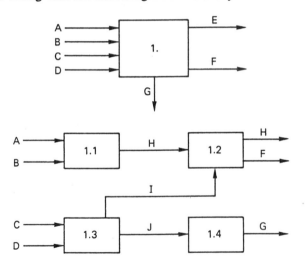

5. You are required to draw a DFD to represent the workings of a manual payroll system run by company X:

Each employee at company X is required to fill in a timesheet for each full day he works. Timesheets are deposited at the end of each day at the data control department. Here the timesheets are checked for accuracy and batched by department.

At the end of the working week the payroll department uses the batched timesheets, together with employee record cards from a payroll file, to calculate the pay for each employee. A two part payslip is produced and passed on to the accounts department. The used timesheets are archived.

The accounts department draw cheques using the information provided on the payslip. A cheque plus part 1 of the payslip is returned to each employee. Part 2 of the payslip is sent to the costing department. This department uses these payslips to produce a number of management reports. Once used, the part 2s are filed in a payroll listing file.

# 7  *Logical Data Dictionaries*

## Introduction

A data dictionary is a means for recording the *metadata* of some organisation; that is, the data about data.

A data dictionary can be considered in at least two ways:

1. *A logical data model.* The purpose of this type of data dictionary is to record and analyse data requirements independently of how these requirements are going to be met.
2. *A physical data model.* The purpose of this type of data dictionary is to record design decisions in terms of database or file structures implemented, and the programs which access them. We might therefore extend our initial definition. A data dictionary is a mechanism for recording the data requirements and data resources of some organisation. This means that a data dictionary need not be considered solely as a tool for the analysis and design of information systems. It may have a number of other uses: for example, training people in data analysis (Maddison and Gawronski, 1985), or as a representation of what we might call a corporate information architecture (see chapter 17).

This chapter will describe in some detail the characteristics of a logical data dictionary. A physical data dictionary, as represented by a software tool known as a data dictionary system or DDS, is discussed in chapter 13.

## The logical view

The logical view details a model of the organisation in terms of a dynamic and static analysis of information requirements. The dynamic view in our terms, involves a collection of descriptions of all the elements included in the set of DFDs used to describe a system – data flows, data stores and processes. The static view details the entities of interest to the enterprise, the relationships between such entities, and indeed, the attributes which define the entities. A conceptual or logical data dictionary is therefore a detailed record of information requirements.

Note that the term data dictionary is stretched to accommodate processes, things which are strictly speaking logic rather than data. Perhaps a data dictionary should really be called something like a 'project directory' or 'information system encyclopedia'. The term data dictionary is, however, in common use, so we shall continue to use it in this chapter.

## Need for a logical data dictionary

Logical data dictionaries have traditionally been associated with DFDs. Data-flow diagrams cannot provide all the information required to specify a system rigorously. For example, they give us very little idea of the composition of flows, processes and stores. Data dictionaries are used to overcome this deficiency; they record additional facts about the data flow in a system in more rigorous and detailed form .

Data dictionaries have also been used as an alternative means for representing entity models. A diagrammatic technique for representing entity models was presented in chapter 5. When E–R diagrams become detailed, however, the information shown on the diagram is more conveniently stored in a data dictionary.

Given that we can represent both flow and structure information, a data dictionary is also a useful means of connecting up the elements involved in a set of with DFDs the elements on a set of E–R diagrams.

We shall examine each of these three uses for a logical data dictionary in this chapter.

## Data structures and data elements

Data flows are data structures in motion; data stores are data structures at rest.                                                                  (Gane, 77)

Data flows and data stores are made up of data structures. A data flow represents the way in which a data structure moves between processes. A data store represents some repository for data structures. A process is designed to transform data structures into other data structures.

A data structure is a set of data elements that are related to one another and which collectively describe some component in a system. For example, an invoice is a classic example of a data structure.

An invoice is made up of a number of items such as invoice number, invoice date and amount due. These are all data elements. A data element, sometimes known as a data item, is hence the smallest and most fundamental unit in an information system.

**Contents of a logical data dictionary**

There is no readily acknowledged standard for the contents of a data dictionary. As a minimum, we could limit ourselves to some description of the data structures used by a system.

Systems analysts often use a special notation to limit the amount of narrative needed to describe relationships between data structures and elements. The one detailed below is a modification of BNF (Backus–Naur Form) – a notation primarily used to define the syntax of programming languages.

| | |
|---|---|
| = | An equals sign means that the item to the left of the sign consists of whatever is indicated on the right. |
| + | A plus sign is equivalent to the word 'and'. |
| [ ... ] | Square brackets means that the item defined contains one and only one of the items in brackets – the notion of selection. Each such contained item is separated by a semi-colon (;). |
| { ... } | Curly braces means that the defined item contains from zero to an infinite number of occurrences of whatever is inside the braces. In other words, they express the concept of iteration. |
| (...) | Information contained in parentheses is optional. That is, zero or one occurrence may appear. |
| *...* | Information between asterisks is comment. That is, it does not constitute part of the definition. |

The simple example below represents a data dictionary for a system emulating the valuation of residential properties. It represents a simple 'syntactic' description of data structures in the valuation system.

```
AGREED-PURCHASE-PRICE    =    * Price provisionally agreed
                                between purchaser and vendor *
BASIC-VALUE       =    * Value produced from valuation-area,
                         property-type, property-age and
                         property-size *
CENTRAL-HEATING  =  CENTRAL-HEATING-TYPE + CENTRAL-HEATING-DEGREE
CENTRAL-HEATING-DEGREE    =    [FULL; PART; NONE]
CENTRAL-HEATING-TYPE      =    [GAS; ELECTRIC; SOLID-FUEL]
CENTRAL-HEATING-FACTOR    =    * Factor to be multiplied against
                                1st-value-range *
DEGREE-OF-REPAIR =    [MAJOR; AVERAGE; MINOR]
FINAL-VALUE       =    HIGH-VALUE + LOW-VALUE
GARAGE    =    [NONE; CONTIGUOUS; DETACHED; DOUBLE]
GARAGE-FACTOR    =    * Factor to be multiplied against
```

```
                           1st-value-range *
LEASE-AMOUNT      =    * Amount in pounds needed to buy lease *
MAINS-SERVICES    =    [FULL; PART; NONE]
MAINS-SERVICES-FACTOR   =   * Factor to be multiplied against
                           1st-value-range *
POUNDS-PER-FOOT   =    * Value per square foot of property *
PRIMARY-FACTORS   =    VALUATION-AREA + PROPERTY-TYPE +
                       PROPERTY-AGE + PROPERTY-SIZE
PROPERTY-AGE      =    [PRE-1ST-WAR; INTER-WAR; POST-WAR; MODERN;
                       NEW]
PROPERTY-SIZE     =    * Size of property in square feet *
PROPERTY-TYPE     =    [END-TERRACED-HOUSE; MID-TERRACED-HOUSE;
                       SEMI-DETACHED-HOUSE; DETACHED-HOUSE;
                       SEMI-DETACHED-BUNGALOW; DETACHED-BUNGALOW;
                       SEMI-DETACHED-DORMER; DETACHED-DORMER]
RECOMMENDATION    =    [UNCONDITIONAL-OFFER; SUBJECT-OFFER;
                       DECLINE]
REPAIR-FACTOR     =    * Factor to be multiplied against
                       1st-value-range *
SECONDARY-FACTORS=     CENTRAL-HEATING + GARAGE +
                       STATE-OF-REPAIR + MAINS-SERVICES
STATE-OF-REPAIR   =    TYPE-OF-REPAIR + DEGREE-OF-REPAIR
TENURE    =    [FREEHOLD; LEASEHOLD]
TYPE-OF-REPAIR    =    [STRUCTURAL; NON-STRUCTURAL; DECORATION]
VALUATION-AREA    =    * Selection from a list of valuation
                       areas for the locality *
VALUATION-AREA-FACTOR   =   [GOOD; UP-COMING; INDIFFERENT;
                       DOWN-GOING; BAD]
1ST-VALUE-RANGE   =    HIGH-VALUE + LOW-VALUE
2ND-VALUE-RANGE   =    HIGH-VALUE + LOW-VALUE
```

## The Gane and Sarson approach

For many purposes, however, what we might call a first-order data dictionary such as represented above is insufficient. A mechanism for representing more completely the information requirements of some organisation is required.

What follows is a description of a data dictionary system as developed by Gane and Sarson (1977) in their book *Structured Systems Analysis*.

In the Gane and Sarson approach, each data flow, data store or process in our set of DFDs must be given a unique, meaningful name which is applied consistently throughout the DFD hierarchy. The first element of a data dictionary in this approach is therefore a list of such names organised to reflect the levelling of our DFD documentation (Weinberg, 1980).

Each element of our 'table of contents' will then have a template sheet of its own describing the element in more detail.

- Data flows. In terms of data flows we might detail the name, a description of the flow, from what process the flow is coming from and to what process it is going to, followed by a list of the data structures used.
- Processes. In terms of processes we have a name and description followed by a list of inbound and outbound data flows. When we reach a sufficient level of detail in our DFDs, we might even include a summary description of the logic of the process in psuedo-code or some other medium (see chapter 9).
- Data stores. Data stores would have a sheet detailing such items as name, description, data flows, and a list of the data stored. If we had sufficient information we might also give some indication of the volume of data and the sort of access required to the data.
- Data structures. When we reach a sufficient level of detail in our DFD system we may seek to document the data structures and elements used by processes, flows and stores.

## Case study: an order processing system

Next we list some extracts from the table of contents of a data dictionary used to describe an order-processing system.

```
Data Stores
-----------
Customer-accounts-receivable
     Customer-name
     Customer-billing-address
     Date-billed
     Amount-billed
     Interest-charges
     Current-balance
Invoice
     Invoice-number
     Customer-name
     Part-number
     Quantity
```

```
        Total-charge
        Delivery-charge
        Total-invoice-charge
Price-list
        Part-number
        Unit-charge
        ..
        ..
        ..


Data Flows
----------
Acknowledgement
        Customer-name
        Customer-billing-address
        Order-acknowledgement
Credit
        Customer-name
        Customer-billing-address
        Credit-amount
Order
        Customer-name
        Customer-billing-address
        Customer-delvery-address
        Customer-part-number
        Quantity
        Delivery-requirements
Statement
        Customer-name
        Customer-billing-address
        Interest-charge
        Total-charge
        ..
        ..


Processes
---------
Enter-order
        Acknowledge-order
        Verify-order
        Approve-order
        File-order
```

```
Produce-invoice
     Prepare-invoice
     File-invoice
Apply-payment-to-invoice
     Post-invoice
     Post-payment
     Approve-credit
     Adjust-account-balance.


     ..
     ..
```

The samples following demonstrate how each of the elements listed in the table of contents can be expanded to provide greater detail.

```
DATA FLOW NAME:    Payment
DESCRIPTION: Cash  or cheques received from  customers  to
                            reduce their account balance.
FROM PROCESSES:    4.1 Enter-settlement
TO PROCESSES:      4.2 Credit-account-balance
DATA STRUCTURES:   Settlement-data
     Payment


DATA FLOW NAME:    Invoice
DESCRIPTION: Details  of  the order and the sum for  which
                            the customer is billed.

FROM PROCESSES:    3.1 Prepare-invoice
TO PROCESSES:      3.2 Assign-invoice-number
DATA STRUCTURES:   Invoice-details
                   Customer-details


PROCESS NAME:      1.0 Enter-order
DESCRIPTION: Customer  order  received  and  approved  for
                            further processing.
INBOUND DATA
FLOWS:      Approved-order
OUTBOUND DATA
FLOWS:      Order-details
```

```
PROCESS NAME: Produce-invoice
DESCRIPTION: Invoice prepared and copies sent to the
             customer and the accounting department.
INBOUND DATA
FLOWS:     Ready-to-ship-details
OUTBOUND DATA
FLOWS:     Invoice


DATA STORE:    Approved-invoices
DESCRIPTION:   Itemises merchandise received,  cost of each and
                          contains signature of receiving employee.
INBOUND DATA
FLOWS: Invoice
OUTBOUND DATA
FLOWS: Batched-invoice-details
DATA DESCRIPTION: Vendor-details, invoice-number, invoice-date,
               Purchase-order-number, item-details, amount-due.
VOLUME: 200 daily
ACCESS: Accessed in batches. Sequentially processed from
                                        within batch.
```

**Data dictionaries for entity models**

Representing an entity model in some form of data dictionary has a number of advantages over its diagrammatic representation. Perhaps the most important is the fact that it is much more amenable to computerisation. An entity model stored on some database system can act as a useful design reference which is easily maintained throughout the life of a project.

We consider here a simple scheme for representing entity models based upon the template approach of Gane and Sarson. Each entity in our system is given a template detailing the entity name and attributes of the entity:

```
ENTITY NAME: customer
IDENTIFIER: customer_no
ATTRIBUTES: customer_name, address, tel_no
```

Each relationship between pairs of entities is described in terms of a name for the relationship and details of participating entities. If a relationship is many-to-many we may also indicate attributes relevant to the relationship:

```
RELATIONSHIP NAME: makes_an_order
ENTITY NAME: customer
DEGREE: 1
MEMBERSHIP: optional
ENTITY NAME: order
DEGREE: N
MEMBERSHIP: mandatory
```

## Connecting up E–R diagrams with DFDs

A data dictionary may act as a useful means for connecting up the static information on a set of E–R diagrams with the dynamic information on a set of DFDs. Probably the easiest way to achieve this integration is to recognise the communality between these two representations in terms of the notion of a data structure. Both data stores and entities are mechanisms for clustering data elements into data structures. Data flows represent data structures in motion, whereas processes are mechanisms for transforming data structures.

Data structure references can hence be transferred between flow and entity models in a data dictionary. A name in the attributes slot of an entity template will then have a correspondence with some name used in a data store, process and flow template elsewhere in the data dictionary. In this way, a data dictionary often acts as the central mechanism in some of the computer-aided software engineering tools (CASE) now available to the systems analyst (see chapter 12). It acts as the bedrock on which graphic interfaces to support techniques such as E–R diagramming and data-flow diagramming can be based.

## Conclusion

Besides its use as an addendum to a set of DFDs, and/or entity models, a data dictionary has a number of other uses in the software development process (see figure 7.1):

1. As a means of enforcing a standard set of data representations for the team undertaking a given software project.
2. As a means of checking the consistency and completeness of our representation of a system.
3. If the dictionary is sufficiently comprehensive and rigorous, generation of machine-readable data definitions and even programs becomes possible.

We might summarise the contents of a data dictionary in BNF as follows:

```
DATA DICTIONARY = CONTENTS LIST + {FLOW  DESCRIPTION} +
                  {STORE DESCRIPTION + PROCESS DESCRIPTION}
FLOW  DESCRIPTION  = FLOW NAME + DESCRIPTION + FROM PROCESS +
                    TO PROCESS + {DATA STRUCTURE}
STORE DESCRIPTION = STORE NAME + DESCRIPTION + {INBOUND DATA FLOW
                    + OUTBOUND DATA FLOW} + DATA DESCRIPTION +
                    (VOLUME + ACCESS)
PROCESS DESCRIPTION = PROCESS NAME + DESCRIPTION + {INBOUND DATA
                      FLOW + OUTBOUND DATA FLOW} + (LOGIC SUMMARY)
DATA STRUCTURE = {DATA ELEMENT}
ENTITY = ENTITY NAME + IDENTIFIER + {ATTRIBUTE}
RELATIONSHIP  =  RELATIONSHIP NAME + {ENTITY NAME + DEGREE +
                 MEMBERSHIP CLASS} + IDENTIFIER + ATTRIBUTE
```

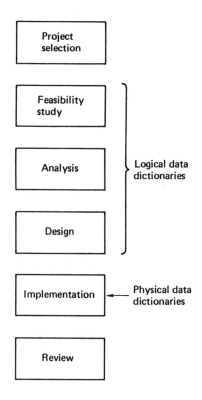

*Figure 7.1*

**Problems**

1. Construct a contents list for the Fast Foods DFD.
2. A clerk within Fast Foods describes an FF invoice as follows: 'Each invoice is given a unique number which we use for indentification. The customer's name and address are indicated at the top of the invoice, and the date of despatch may be written on by the despatch handler. Underneath the customer information we list for each product ordered the product number, product description, quantity ordered, unit price, and value of order. At the bottom of the invoice we write the total value of the order.' Write a modified BNF description for the FF invoice.
3. Construct a process template for the despatch goods process on the Fast Foods DFD.
4. What is wrong with the following data dictionary entry? TOTAL ITEM PRICE = UNIT PRICE + VAT

# 8 Entity Life Histories

## Introduction

The entity life history (ELH) technique was originally designed as an attempt to extend the available database design techniques such as E–R diagramming and normalisation (Robinson, 1979). Such 'data analysis' techniques concentrate almost exclusively on a static view of the information system being modelled.

ELHs in contrast were developed as a method for the explicit modelling of system dynamics (Rosenquist, 1982). In a sense, the ELH was originally designed to be a competitor to the DFD, but a technique obviously more closely linked to the logical modelling ideas underlying data analysis (Rock Evans, 1981).

Recently however, a number of methodologies have cast the ELH in a more integrative role; mediating between such techniques as E–R diagrams and DFDs (Cutts, 1987). Michael Jackson has even used a similar representation to the one that we shall be using as the basis of his structured programming methodology (Jackson, 1975) (see chapter 10.).

## Definition and objectives

From a traditional modelling point of view, the entities that we have considered in our discussion of E–R diagramming are usually thought of as static. An E–R diagram is a static model of the 'real world'. It represents a time-independent slice of reality.

An entity may however be considered from a contrasting point of view. An entity is realistically in a state of flux. It is the subject of a large number of processes or events which change its state. In a library, for instance, the entity Book may go through a number of states: it is first acquired, then it is catalogued, it is lent to borrowers, and perhaps finally it is sold off.

An ELH is a diagrammatic technique for charting the usage of a particular entity by the processes or events making up an information system. Its primary objective is therefore to offer a means to connect up the entities detailed on E–R diagrams, with the processes present on the set of system DFDs.

As a result, ELHs are useful in that they help analysts to understand entities better. They are also the first step in documenting the detailed outline of processes and, as such, are an extremely useful technique for the validation of DFDs.

## Technique

There are at least three different diagramming conventions used in drawing ELHs (Cutts, 1987):
1. A notation based on the theory of Petri nets (Martin, 1985).
2. A network-like notation derived from PERT scheduling.
3. A hierarchical convention similar to the symbols used in JSP (Jackson Structured Program Design) which we shall discuss in chapter 10 (Jackson, 1975).

Each of these conventions incorporates the basic characteristics of the ELH as an analysis and design tool. Primarily for the sake of brevity , therefore, we choose to concentrate on describing the hierarchical notation. Those interested in the Petri net and network notations are referred to (Cutts, 1987) and (Martin and McClure, 1985).

The generation of any set of ELH's is a four step process:
1. List entities from E–R diagrams.
2. List events or processes from DFDs.
3. Construct an ELH or function matrix.
4. Produce an ELH for each entity.

Let us consider each one of these stages in turn.

### List entities

The entities used in a set of ELHs are usually taken directly from an entity-relationship diagram or diagrams. Hence, in a simple library system we might have the following entities:
Book
Borrower
Reservation
Loan

## List events

Events are usually taken from the set of DFDs documenting an information system. An event can be thought of as a real-world transaction, such as the arrival of a sales order or the receipt of goods. The net effect of an event is to change the state of an entity. Hence, we might say that a catalogue event changes the state of a Book entity from 'acquired' to 'catalogued'. Events can,however, be categorised in a more abstract sense by the effect that they have on the entity – create events (C), read events (R), amend events (A) or delete events (D).

A list of possible events for our simple library system might be:

Creating a borrower
Acquiring a book
Cataloguing a book
Loaning a book
Selling a book
Reserving a book

## Construct an ELH matrix

A two-dimensional matrix can then be produced in which entries in the cells indicate the action of an event on an entity. An example is given below.

|                   | Book | Borrower | Reservation | Loan |
|-------------------|------|----------|-------------|------|
| Create a borrower |      | C        |             |      |
| Acquire a book    | C    |          |             |      |
| Catalogue a book  | A    |          |             |      |
| Loan a book       | A    | A        | D           | C    |
| Reserve a book    | R    |          | C           | A    |
| Sell a book       | D    |          |             |      |

Key: C - Create
     A - Amend
     D - Delete
     R - Read

## Constructing an ELH diagram

An ELH matrix suffers first from its inability to indicate for every entity the sequence of events, and second, from its inability to detail the effect of abnormal events. ELHs are drawn to overcome these inadequacies: they chart the sequence of events in an entity's life, and the effect of abnormal events.

ELH diagrams in our notation are made up of a hierarchical system of boxes. The top-level box indicates the name of the entity under consideration. The lower-level boxes represent the events or processes that act upon the entity. ELH diagrams also use three basic constructs similar to those used in Jackson diagrams (Jackson,1975) (see figure 8.1):

1. Sequence: represented by a horizontal row of boxes read from left to right.
2. Selection: represented by boxes at the same level with an 'O' (for optional) symbol within each box.
3. Iteration: represented by boxes with an asterisk '*' symbol.

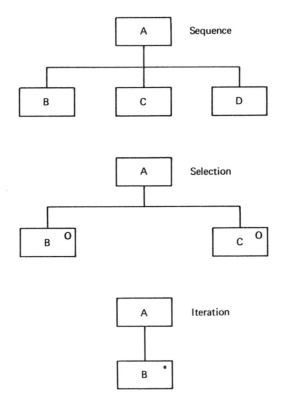

*Figure 8.1*

### Creation of ELHs

The easiest way to construct an ELH is to start with a simple entity life first and add complexities later. Many entities have simple lives in which an entity occurrence is created, read and/or modified a number of times, and eventually deleted. In our library system for instance, a book is first created by an acquisition process, it is then modified by a cataloging and lending process, and finally deleted by a process which sells off old books (see figure 8.2).

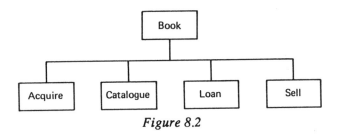

*Figure 8.2*

A complexity arises when we consider that a book is likely to be loaned a number of times throughout its life. We therefore demote the loan box to a position underneath a box which we now label 'library life', and we designate a loan as involving iteration. Similarly, we break down the acquisition process into the sub-processes 'order', 'receive' and 'payment' (see figure 8.3).

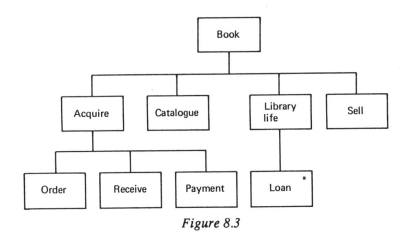

*Figure 8.3*

Further complexities occur if we consider the loan event in greater detail. The loan of a book actually involves two separate processes which we label 'issues' and 'returns'. The issuing process is relatively straightforward. We record details of the borrower and book, we stamp the book with a return date, and we issue the book to the borrower. Returns are a little more complex. Most returns will, we hope, take place before or on the return date, but inevitably some books will run overdue. In this case, we issue as many return requests as it takes to get the book returned (see figure 8.4).

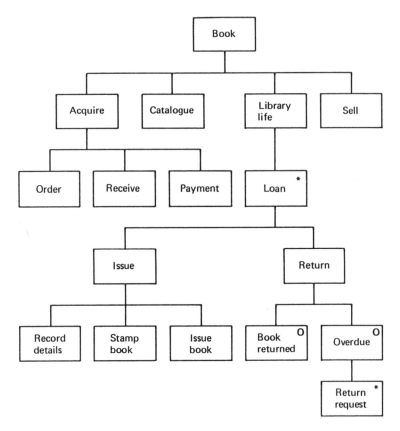

*Figure 8.4*

This is clearly not the end of the story. The life history needs to be elaborated further to provide an accurate picture of the Book entity's dynamics. This is, however, left as an exercise for the reader.

**Conclusion**

We might therefore describe a sequence of steps for the generation of ELHs as follows:

1. Select from the ELH matrix an entity and the events that affect it.
2. Order the events in sequence.
3. Include selections and iterations.
4. Rework the ELH if the iterations or selections alter the sequence.

As an aid to E–R diagramming and perhaps data-flow diagramming, ELHs can be used at the feasibility study, analysis and design stages of the project life cycle. Jackson has used a similar technique as a tool for deriving appropriate program structures. In this sense, ELHs might also be seen as relevant to the implementation phase (figure 8.5).

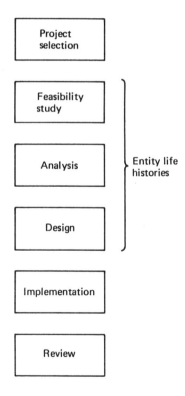

*Figure 8.5*

**Problems**

1. Consider a customer in an order-processing system. The event that makes the system aware of the customer in the first place is one whereby the customer notifies the system of his address etc. During the customer's active life he might place orders, take deliveries, be invoiced and make payments. Assume that the only reason the warehouse may lose a customer is if he goes out of business. Draw a simple life for this system.

2. In an order processing system such as Fast Foods, an order entity is first created by an order entry process, then modified by a function which produces a delivery note and invoice, and finally deleted by a process which receives the payment of invoice. Draw an ELH to represent this simple life.

3. Combine the the ELH from problem 2 with the ELH from problem 1.

4. A new customer opening an account with Fast Foods may negotiate a discount. Occasionally, customers will move to new premises. Some of the customers seem to be doing very well, in that they are frequently moving to bigger premises. The discount rate that is offered to a customer is dependent on the delivery distance, so when a customer moves premises Fast Foods are prepared to renegotiate a new discount rate. The old discount rate is used until the new one is negotiated. Incorporate this analysis into the ELH produced from problem 3.

# 9   Process Descriptions

## Introduction

Any information system can be described in terms of three major components: data flows, data structures and processes. Data flows have been the subject of our chapters on DFDs and data dictionaries. Data structures have been discussed using normalisation and E–R diagramming. The third component, processes, are the subject of this chapter.

One of the major reasons for using a structured approach to systems development is the need to remove ambiguities from system descriptions. Such ambiguities frequently arise in the natural language description of processes. For this reason, structured systems development exploits three major methods for describing processes which are less subject to ambiguity:

1. Structured English/pseudo-code
2. Decision tables
3. Decision trees

Structured English puts verbal descriptions into a form which removes logical ambiguities. This has two benefits: the structure removes logical ambiguities, but English narrative can still be used to describe activities.

Decision tables and decision trees are preferred to structured English where one of a large number of actions is to be selected, or where a large number of conditions contribute to the actions undertaken.

Other techniques such as Warnier–Orr diagrams and action diagrams are also used in process description. Since the principles discussed here are equally relevant to Warnier–Orr and action diagrams, however, no attempt is made to discuss these notations in this chapter. Readers interested in these techniques are referred to Martin and McClure (1985).

## Structured English and pseudo-code

The logical constructs of structured English are a direct emulation of the constructs of structured programming. Descriptions written in structured English therefore look very similar to programs written in block-structured languages such as Pascal and Modula-2. Some people make a distinction between two types of description written in this vein: structured English and pseudo-code. A description written in structured English is, if you like, an attempt at logical description. As such, it should remain as high-level or as general as possible. When implementation details become important such descriptions are said to be written in pseudo-code. Pseudo-code descriptions are physical descriptions; it is a very small step from a pseudo-code description to a program.

The distinction is very hazy. Another way of looking at it is that structured English is primarily a tool to be used in the analysis of systems. Pseudo-code, in contrast, is a tool to be used in the design of information systems.

A structured English description of any process is likely to be made up of blocks of imperative sentences embedded within suitable control structures. Let us examine each of these components in turn.

**Imperative sentences**

An imperative sentence is usually made up of a verb followed by a number of data items. For example:

READ sales_record FROM sales

The data items referred to in the sentence are usually expected to reference in some way the data flows and data stores on a DFD used to describe a system. Hence in our example 'sales_record' is probably a data flow while 'sales' is probably a data store.

It is also usual to group a logical collection of imperative sentences into a 'block' delineated by the keywords BEGIN and END. For example, the block below decribes the process of handling sale-slips:

```
HANDLE_SALES

    BEGIN
            receive sales_slip
            READ customer_record from customers
            READ product_record from products
            total_sale_value = qty_sold * unit_price
            customer_credit = customer_credit + total_sale_value
            update customer_credit on customer_record
            create sales_record
            create advice_note
            WRITE customer_record TO customers
            WRITE sales_record TO sales
            send advice_note to customer
    END
```

Note also that we provide a name for each process description. Such names will usually refer to templates within a data dictionary as described in chapter 7.

### Control structures

According to the advocates of structured programming (Dahl, et al., 1972), it appears that only three control structures are needed to describe any process:

### 1. The sequence

This is the simplest control structure in which each statement is executed sequentially. For example,

```
HANDLE_ORDERS
BEGIN
    READ stock_record FROM stock
    qty_in_stock = qty_in_stock - order_qty
    update stock_record
    WRITE stock_record TO stock
END
```

### 2. The condition

This is the control structure which allows us to deal with a number of different situations in different ways. Without the condition structure, a different description would be needed to handle every minor variation in the specification of a problem. Conditions can be subdivided into three types:

*Single-branched*
IF condition THEN action ENDIF. For example,

```
HANDLE_ORDERS
BEGIN
     receive order
     read customer_record from customers
     IF credit_rating is 'good' THEN
          BEGIN
               READ stock_record FROM stock
               qty_in_stock = qty_in_stock - order_qty
               update stock_record
               WRITE stock_record TO stock
          END
     ENDIF
     create invoice
     send stock and invoice to customer
END
```

### Double-branched

```
IF condition THEN action
ELSE action.
ENDIF
```

### For example,

```
HANDLE_ORDERS
BEGIN
     receive order
     read customer_record from customers
     IF credit_rating is 'good' THEN
          BEGIN
               READ stock_record FROM stock
               qty_in_stock = qty_in_stock - order_qty
               update stock_record
               WRITE stock_record TO stock
               create invoice
               send stock and invoice to customer
          END
     ELSE
          BEGIN
               create request_for_payment
               send request_for_payment to customer
          END
     ENDIF
END
```

## *Multi-branched*

```
CASE condition
     action
CASE condition
     action
CASE condition
     action
ENDCASE
```

## For example:

```
HANDLE_ORDERS

BEGIN
     receive order
     read customer_record from customers
     CASE credit_rating is 'good'
          BEGIN
               READ stock_record FROM stock
               qty_in_stock = qty_in_stock - order_qty
               update stock_record
               WRITE stock_record TO stock
               create invoice
               send stock and invoice to customer
          END
     CASE credit_rating is 'average'
          BEGIN
               create request_for_payment
               send request_for_payment to customer
          END
     CASE credit_rating is 'bad'
          BEGIN
               create settlement_request
               send settlement_request to customer
          END
     ENDCASE
END
```

### The loop

The loop is an important control structure in that it permits the analyst to repeat a series of operations without the need to duplicate the necessary descriptions. There are three types of looping structure popular in languages such as Pascal:

*Looping while a condition is true*

```
WHILE condition
     action
       ..
ENDWHILE
```

For instance, we might nest the process description above in a while loop as follows.

```
WHILE there are more orders
     BEGIN
          DO HANDLE_ORDERS
     END
ENDWHILE
```

*Looping until a condition is met*

```
REPEAT
       action
       ..
UNTIL condition
```

```
REPEAT
     BEGIN
          DO HANDLE_ORDERS
     END
UNTIL there are no more orders
```

The major difference between a while loop and a repeat..until loop is that the repeat..until loop must execute at least once.

*Looping a fixed number of times*

```
FOR number of times
    action
    ..
NEXT
```

For instance, suppose in our system we batch orders together in bundles of 100 for processing. The following description might then be appropriate.

```
FOR 100 orders
    BEGIN
        DO HANDLE_ORDERS
    END
NEXT order
```

## Guidelines in writing structured English

1. Avoid complexity. The aim is to achieve process descriptions that can be readily understood. One rule of thumb is that a structured description of some process should not exceed one page in length. If it does, then the process probably needs additional levelling.
2. Use and capitalise accepted keywords such as IF, THEN, ELSE, WHILE, REPEAT, FOR.
3. Indent blocks of sentences to show their structure clearly.

## Decision tables and decision trees

Processes involving multiple nested decisions are difficult to describe using structured English. For this class of problems, two other techniques, namely decision tables and decision trees, are more appropriate.

Let us assume, for instance, that the process of admitting people to a zoological garden can be described in natural language as follows:

A child under 3 years of age is not to be charged an admission fee. A person under 18 is to be charged half full admission. If a child under 12 is accompanied by an adult, however, then that person is to be charged quarter full admission. For persons over 18 full admission is to be charged, except for students who are to be charged half admission and senior citizens (women over 60; men over 65) who are to be charged quarter full admission. A discount of 10% is to apply to all persons subject to full admission who are members of a party of 10 or more. Finally, there are no student concessions on the weekend.

## Decision tables

Figure 9.1 represents a decision table solution to the admissions problem expressed above. A decision table is made up of four parts:

1. The conditions stub which indicates in a number of rows the appropriate questions to be asked. This is the top left section of the decision table.
2. The conditions entry which indicates in a series of columns the appropriate combination of conditions that apply. This is the top right section.
3. The actions stub which indicates in a series of rows the appropriate actions to be taken in a process. This is the bottom left section.
4. The actions entry which indicates in a series of columns the appropriate combination of actions that apply, given the combination of conditions. This is the bottom right section.

The decision table in figure 9.1 is an example of an extended decision table. The simpler form of decision table merely has yes (Y) or no (N) values in the condition entry section of the table. In the admissions problem however age is obviously a crucial factor. Age cannot be handled in a logical yes–no way but must use some form of continuous or discrete scale of values.

Condition Stub:                                    Condition Entry:

| | | | | | | | | | |
|---|---|---|---|---|---|---|---|---|---|
| AGE | LT 3 | 3-12 | 3-12 | 12-18 | 18+ | 18+ | 18+ | 18+ | 18+ SC |
| ACCOMPANIMENT | | Y | N | | | | | | |
| STUDENT | | | | | Y | Y | Y | N | N |
| WEEKEND | | | | | N | Y | Y | | |
| PARTY MEMBER | | | | | | Y | N | Y | N |

Action Stub:                                       Action Entry:

| | | | | | | | | | |
|---|---|---|---|---|---|---|---|---|---|
| FREE | X | | | | | | | | |
| QUARTER | | X | | | | | | | |
| HALF | | | X | X | X | | | | X |
| 90% | | | | | | X | | X | |
| FULL | | | | | | | X | | X |

*Figure 9.1*

## Decision trees

Figure 9.2 represents a decision tree for the same admissions problem. The decision tree defines the conditions as a sequence of left to right tests. We first ask the age of the person. If the person is over 18 but not a senior citizen we ask whether that person is a student. If he or she is a student we ask whether it is a weekend or not, and so on. Each node of the tree is therefore a question; each branch of the tree constitutes an action. A conclusion is reached at the terminal node of the tree.

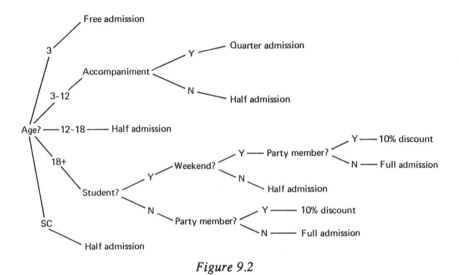

*Figure 9.2*

## Conclusion

This chapter has introduced only three representations for process logic out of a large variety of representations available. A major question remains: how does an analyst judge which is the best representation for the job? There are no firm conclusions to be drawn, but some guidelines are presented below:

1. Use structured English when there are many repetitive actions or when communication to end-users is important.
2. Use decision tables when complex combinations of conditions and actions are found in the problem. Decision tables are also good for avoiding logical contradictions in the representation of a problem.

3. Use decision trees when the sequence of conditions and actions is crucial or when not every condition is relevant to every action.

As we discussed above, process descriptions are generally held to be applicable to the analysis and design phases of the project life-cycle. They are also used within the implementation phase, perhaps in the form of program specifications, but this is not their primary purpose (figure 9.3).

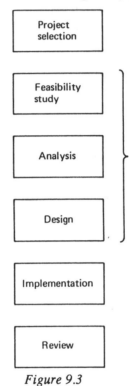

*Figure 9.3*

## Problems

1. Identify the ambiguities in the following English sentence: All customers with more than £1000 in their deposit account who have an average monthly balance in their current account of £100 or who have been customers of the bank for more than 5 years are entitled to free banking services.
2. Write a structured English sentence for each of the possible meanings of the sentence in problem 1.

3. What are the advantages of the structured English representation as compared to a natural language sentence?

4. Draw a decision table and a decision tree for the following problem:

Shady Sellers operate a graded commission policy for their salesmen. The company makes a rough distinction between items selling at more than £10000 and items selling at under £10000. Items above £10000 are subject to a commission of 16% if more than 500 items are sold and the salesman's salary is below £12000. Salaries in the region £12–20000 gain 14% commission, and salaries above £20000 gain 12% commission. If less than 500 items are sold then the commission is 8%, 7% and 6% for the same classification of salesmen. For items having a value under £10000 the situation changes. Sales over 1000 items gain a 12% commission for staff on salaries under £12000. Those on £12–20000 get 11%, and those on £20000 plus get 8%. Under 1000 items gain a 6%, 5% and 4% commission respectively.

5. Which method of process description is most appropriate for the Shady Sellers problem?

6. Represent the rules for transforming an E–R diagram into a set of table structures (as described in chapter 5) as a series of structured English sentences.

# 10 Structured Program Design

## Introduction

In previous chapters we have concentrated on a range of techniques applicable in the analysis and design of information systems. In this chapter we begin to concentrate on implementation. We discuss a number of techniques applicable to the process of program design.

Program design can be described as the process whereby the requirements defined in the documentation of a system are turned into a representation close to actual code. Since the essential role of program requirements is to show how for each process input is transformed into output, the program design process may be represented schematically as follows (Daniels, 1984):

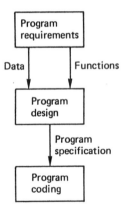

From this diagram it is obvious that two basic alternative approaches to structured program design are possible. One approach based on functional decomposition has been promulgated by, for example, Myers, Constantine and Yourdon in the USA (Yourdon and Constantine, 1979). The other, data-oriented approach has been represented by Jackson (1975) and Warnier (1981) in the UK and France respectively. In this chapter we present merely an overview of both these techniques as an illustration of the available methods of program implementation. Readers wishing to know more about either approach are referred to the works cited above.

## The functional approach

In the late 1970s Edward Yourdon and Larry Constantine published a very influential book entitled *Structured Design: Fundamentals of a Discipline of Computer Program and System Design* (Yourdon and Constantine, 1979). The major theme of this work was that the fundamental problem with software is complexity. Yourdon and Constantine introduced a number of principles for handling such complexity which they bundled together under the term structured design. Structured design seeks to conquer the complexity of large systems in two ways:

1. Partitioning a system into black boxes
2. Organising these black boxes hierarchically

### *Partitioning the system into black boxes*

A black box is a software module in which:

1. The inputs to the module can be clearly specified
2. The outputs from the module can be specified
3. Its function can be clearly specified; that is, what it does to the inputs to achieve the outputs
4. One does not need to know how the module carries out its function in order to use it

There are a number of advantages in using the black-box approach. Black-box systems are easily:

1. constructed
2. tested
3. corrected
4. understood
5. modified

The principles of the black-box approach are as follows:

1. Each black box should solve one well-defined piece of the problem.
2. The system should be partitioned so that the function of each black box is easy to understand.
3. Partitioning should be such that any connection between boxes is introduced only because of a connection between pieces of the problem.
4. Partitioning should assume that the connections between black boxes are as simple as possible.

*Organising the black boxes into hierarchies*

It is useful to make the analogy between the structure of a computer system and the structure of a business organisation in order to suggest some general guidelines for the design of information systems.

1. A manager module should not have more than seven immediate subordinates reporting to it (Miller, 1967).
2. Work and management should be separated in the system. Work should be done by the subordinates with no managerial duties. Manager modules should be restricted to coordinating the work of subordinates.
3. Every department in the company should have a well-defined function:
   (a) Every job should be allocated to the proper department.
   (b) Reports should be readable, clear and meaningfully laid out.
   (c) A manager should give only as much information to a subordinate as that person needs to do his job.

The analogy is useful in emphasising that most viable information systems are subject to some form of restricted hierarchy. Control in the system is vested in the upper regions of the hierarchy. Work in the system is done at the lowest levels. Communication between the components of the system is through well-defined channels using simple messages.

## Qualities of good design

Hierarchy is therefore one criterion to be used in assessing the quality of an information system design. Yourdon and Constantine however provide two other concepts to be used to assess the quality of any software design: coupling and cohesion.

*Coupling*

Coupling is a measure of the degree of interdependence between modules. The objective of good systems design is to minimise coupling; that is, to make modules as independent as possible. Low coupling indicates a well-partitioned system. We want low coupling because:

1. The fewer connections there are between two modules, the less chance there is of the so-called 'ripple effect' – a bug in one module appearing as a symptom in another.

2. We want to be able to change one module with the minimum risk of having to change another module, and we want each change to affect as few modules as possible.
3. While maintaining one module, we do not want to worry about the internal workings of another module.

Low coupling can be obtained in three general ways:

1. By eliminating unnecessary relationships between modules.
2. By reducing the number of necessary relationships.
3. By easing the 'tightness' of necessary relationships.

Yourdon and Constantine have detailed five major categories of coupling that may occur between modules. They are described in terms of their degree of 'tightness':

1. Data coupling                    Good (loose)
2. Stamp coupling
3. Control coupling
4. Common coupling
5. Content coupling                 Bad (tight)

Good or loose coupling occurs if two modules communicate solely by parameters, each parameter being either a single field or table. Data coupling constitutes the necessary communication of data between modules and is hence unavoidable. The other forms of coupling however violate the black-box nature of the modules involved and can be avoided. For instance, two modules are said to be common-coupled if they refer to the same global data area. Common-coupling is dangerous for a number of reasons, the most important of which is the tendency to exhibit the 'ripple effect' discussed above.

### Cohesion

Cohesion is a function of how closely the elements within a single module are related to one another. What we want are strong, highly cohesive modules – modules whose elements are strongly and genuinely related together.

Clearly coupling and cohesion are interrelated in that the greater cohesion within the individual modules of a system, the lower the coupling between the modules should be.

Yourdon and Constantine have developed a scale of cohesion as a measure of the black-box nature of a module:

1. Functional          Best maintainability
2. Sequential
3. Communicational
4. Procedural
5. Temporal
6. Logical
7. Coincidental        Worst maintainability

A functionally cohesive module contains elements that all contribute to the execution of one, and only one, problem-related task. The following are probably examples of functionally cohesive modules:

- Read transaction record
- Determine customer mortgage repayment
- Calculate net employee salary

A temporally cohesive module is one whose elements are involved activities that are related together in time. The classic example of temporal cohesion is an initialisation module. The problem with such a module is that it is difficult to reuse. If the module involved such diverse activities as clearing tables and rewinding tapes, it is impossible to reinitialise any one tape without resetting the entire system.

### DFDs and design

Data-flow diagrams can be used as the first stage of the design process. That is, as the initial input to the modular formation of a piece of software. Yourdon and Constantine (1979) have demonstrated a way of moving from DFDs to structured programs via a notation that they call structure charts. A structure chart is a graphic tool for representing the hierarchical structure of a system. A structure chart is made up of three basic elements (figure 10.1):

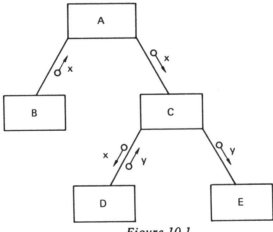

*Figure 10.1*

- The module: a named, bounded, contiguous set of statements, represented by a labelled, rectangular box.

```
┌──────────┐
│          │
│          │
├──────────┘
│ Label    │
└──────────┘
```

- The connection: any reference from one module to something defined in another module. It usually means that one module has called the other. It is represented by a directed arrow or line joining two modules.

─────────────

- The couple: a data item that moves from one module to another. It is represented by a short arrow with a circular tail. A dotted tail means an element of control is involved, while a small open circle means that an element of data is being passed between two modules.

A DFD is a statement of requirement. It declares what has to be accomplished. A structure chart is a statement of design: it declares how the requirement is to be met. Design must therefore somehow be derived from requirement in the sense that we arrive at an appropriate structure chart from a corresponding DFD. Yourdon and Constantine indicate two methods for such derivation: transform analysis and transaction analysis. These two methods deal with two different kinds of DFDs or portions thereof. The main objective of transform analysis is to identify the primary processing functions of the system. In contrast, transaction analysis applies to those cases where a transform splits an input data stream into several discrete output streams. Transform analysis is undoubtedly the technique applicable to more systems than transaction analysis. We will therefore concentrate on this technique in the present chapter.

**Transform analysis**

Transform analysis involves the following steps:

1. Restate the problem as a DFD. Figure 10.2a is an idealised data-flow diagram that we wish to transform into a structure chart.
2. Identify high-level inputs and high-level outputs.

   High-level inputs are those elements of data that are furthest removed from physical input, yet still constitute inputs to the system (Yourdon and Constantine, 1979).

   To identify high-level inputs, we start at physical inputs to the system and move inward along the flows of the DFD until we identify a stream that can no longer be considered as incoming. We perform this for each input stream.

   High-level outputs are those data elements that are furthest removed from physical outputs but which still may be regarded as outgoing (Yourdon and Constantine, 1979).

   To identify high level outputs, we start at physical outputs and perform a similar process to the above.

   These steps usually leave a set of processes (transforms) in the middle. These are designated the central transforms of the system. They constitute the main work of the system: they transform major inputs into major outputs. Process 2 has been designated the central transform on figure 10.2a.

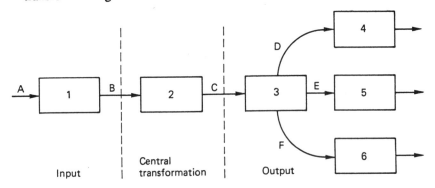

*Figure 10.2a*

3. First-level factoring. Having identified the central transform, we now begin the process of constructing the structure chart. All such charts begin with a top-level control module which we shall call the executive

module. Underneath this executive we need three lower level modules: one module to get the B data flow; one module to transform B into C; and one module to output C. Figure 10.2b represents this first level factoring of the DFD in figure 10.2a.

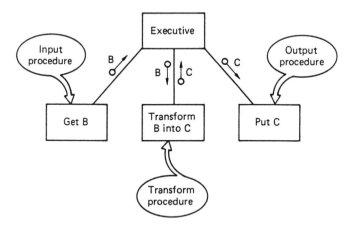

*Figure 10.2b*

4. Lower-level factoring. We continue this factoring process until we are sure that we have adequately represented the problem. Figure 10.3 represents the factoring of the get B module. Figure 10.4 represents the factoring of the put C module.

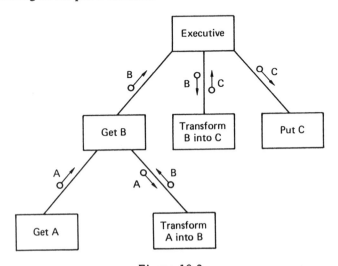

*Figure 10.3*

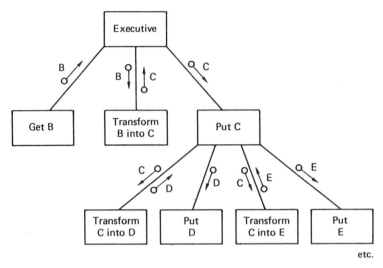

*Figure 10.4*

**Case study: an examinations system**

The diagram in figure 10.5 describes the data flow through a system for handling student examination results. Sets of examination marks are first read from an examination results file and validated. Invalid marks are written to an invalid marks file, and statistics of the number of sets of valid and invalid marks are kept.

The valid marks are then processed to determine the relevant student grades in each subject, and the overall grade for the course. Marks and grades for each student are recorded on a student's records file. An individual results sheet is also produced for each student, and an entry is made in the overall course results sheet.

Our task is to transform this network representation for the examinations system into a more hierarchical representation, namely a structure chart. The first step is to identify the central transform or transforms for the system. That is, the processes which perform the basic functions of the system – turning inputs into outputs. In our example, these are the processes labelled 'determine subject grades' and 'determine overall course grade'. In more complex, and perhaps more realistic situations, identification of the central transform usually requires considerable analysis. Indeed, different

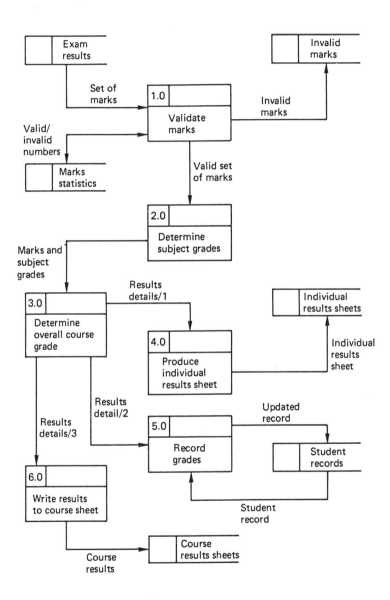

*Figure 10.5*

analysts working independently might identify different processes as being the central transform.

The second step is to identify those data flows which input data to the main processes, and distribute data from the main processes. These are called the afferent and efferent data flows. In our example, the 'valid set of marks' data flow is the afferent data flow. The 'valid set of marks', 'subject grades' and 'overall course grade' are the efferent data flows.

The structure chart is then produced by first defining a controlling module or executive which controls the processing, input, and output of data (Process exam results). Underneath this 'executive' we draw a data collection module (Obtain set of valid results), a processing module (Analyse marks), and an output module (Disseminate results) (figure 10.6).

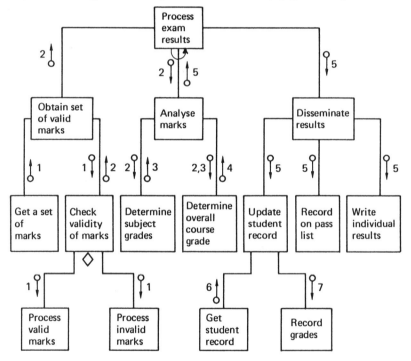

Key: 1 — Set of marks
2 — Valid marks
3 — Subject grades
4 — Overall course grade
5 — 2, 3, 4
6 — Student record
7 — Updated student record

*Figure 10.6*

These three modules in turn control further modules at lower levels in the hierarchy which perform subordinate processes. What we are effectively doing here is moving out from the central transform and afferent and efferent flows to incorporate other parts of the data-flow diagram.

The sequence of execution of the various modules making up the structure chart is from left to right. Iteration is shown on the chart by a circular arrow. In our example, the circular arrow indicates that the three top-level modules are to be repeated. Selection can also be indicated by the use of a diamond. On our structure chart, the module (Check validity of marks) has the choice of either performing the (Process valid marks) module or the (Process invalid marks) module.

It remains to further annotate the structure chart with the data couples that are passed between modules. The emphasis in structured design is on the use of data couples as opposed to control couples. It is possible, for instance, to incorporate the functions of the (Process valid marks) and (Process invalid marks) modules into one module. A countrol flag would then need to be passed to this module by the CHECK VALIDITY OF MARKS module to indicate which function is to be carried out in any particular case. The existence of control parameters, however, results in a high degree of coupling between modules. This in turn leads to increased program amendment problems.

The resulting structure chart is thus an example of good software design. It is characterised by low coupling between modules and high cohesion within modules. Each module comprises a black box, in that it is a simple module that performs one function well. The only communication between modules is through data couples. Control is exercised appropriately at various levels in the hierarchy and involves a simple calling of appropriate procedures. All these characteristics lead to systems that are easy to understand, construct and maintain.


## Data-oriented program design

The basic premise of data-oriented program design is that the structure of the data determines the structure of the program. Probably the best known and certainly the best documented structured program design methodology was developed by M.Jackson in the early to mid-1970s (Jackson, 1975). Jackson Structured Programming (JSP) was subsequently chosen as a standard for all UK government installations as Structured Design Methodology (SDM).

### Structure diagrams

Given the basic premise of designing programs from data, Jackson needs a notation to represent both data structures and program structures. Jackson uses a hierarchical diagram, called a structure diagram, to represent both.

For any programming problem, structure diagrams may be drawn consisting of three basic constructs, identical to those used in the chapter on entity life histories (figure 10.7):

1. Sequence.
2. Iteration (loop).
3. Selection (choice).

Jackson's structure diagram looks very similar to the structure chart proposed by Yourdon and Constantine. When used to show program structure, the structure diagram and the structure chart give the same information with the following exceptions: only the structure chart shows data passing between modules, and only the structure diagram can effectively show the control constructs of selection and iteration.

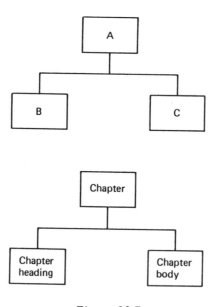

*Figure 10.7a*

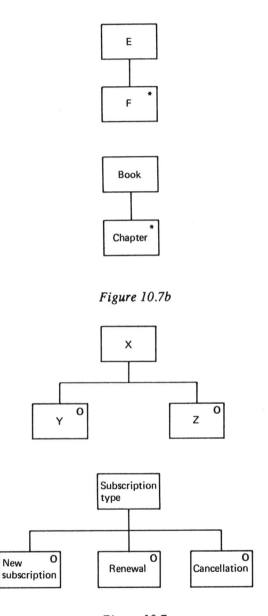

*Figure 10.7b*

*Figure 10.7c*

## Stages of JSP

JSP comprises five distinct stages performed in sequence.

1. Draw a separate data structure for each input and output in the problem.
2. Identify correspondences between data structures.
3. Use these correspondences to combine separate data structures into a single program structure.
4. List the executable operations and allocate them to appropriate places within the program structure.
5. Write schematic logic for the program.

### Case study: a simple banking program

Let us assume that we are given the following simple problem:

A program is required to process a file containing a series of transactions in account number sequence to produce a printed summary report for a manager. In addition to the account number, each transaction record contains the amount of the transaction in pounds, and an indicator to represent whether the transaction is a 'credit' or a 'debit'. The summary report is to be headed 'account summary' and is to have one line per account showing the total value of transactions for each account.

A context DFD for this system might therefore be drawn as in figure 10.8. Our input data flow is the file of transactions; our output data flow is the summary report. The first step in JSP is to draw structure diagrams for both of these flows. Two such diagrams are presented in figure 10.8.

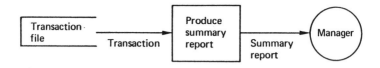

*Figure 10.8*

The second step is to identify correspondences between these data structures. For correspondences to exist, the following conditions must be satisfied:

1. Each item in the data structures must occur the same number of times.
2. The items must be in the same sequence.

In our example, File corresponds with Report, since there is only one of each for each program execution. Similarly, there is a correspondence between Account and Account line. Having identified correspondences, we indicate them by drawing a double-headed arrow between corresponding components as in figure 10.9.

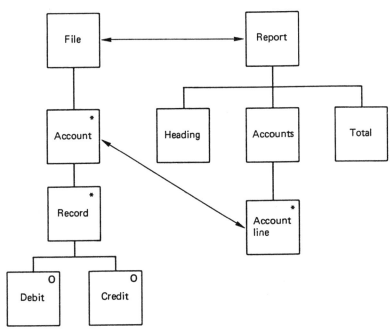

*Figure 10.9*

The third step in JSP involves taking the corresponding component data structures and combining them into a single box in the program structure. Then the non-corresponding boxes are taken from each data structure and added to the program structure in turn whilst preserving the original hierarchy, as in figure 10.10.

The fourth step is to list program operations such as terminating the program, opening and closing files, performing calculations, reading records etc. Having listed the operations, the next step is to allocate them to appropriate points in the program structure. Strictly speaking, operations can only be allocated to sequence components, and this may entail the addition of 'dummy' boxes to the program structure. Two questions have to be asked for each operation in turn:

1. With which component box or boxes is the operation associated?
2. Whereabouts in the sequence does it belong – beginning, end or elsewhere?

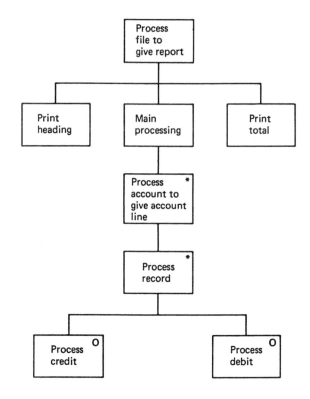

*Figure 10.10*

| A) | 1) | stop |
|----|----|------|
| B) | 2) | open FILE, REPORT |
|    | 3) | close FILE, REPORT |
| C) | 4) | print title |
|    | 5) | print account line |
|    | 6) | print total |
| D) | 7) | ACCOUNT = ACCOUNT + CREDIT |
|    | 8) | ACCOUNT = ACCOUNT - DEBIT |
|    | 9) | TOTAL = TOTAL + ACCOUNT |
| E) | 10) | read FILE record |
| F) | 11) | ACCOUNT = 0 |
|    | 12) | TOTAL = 0 |
|    | 13) | store account number |

The fifth step is to write schematic logic or structured text (figure 10.11). Schematic logic is a language-independent pseudo-code designed to translate the program structure diagram into a form more amenable to coding.

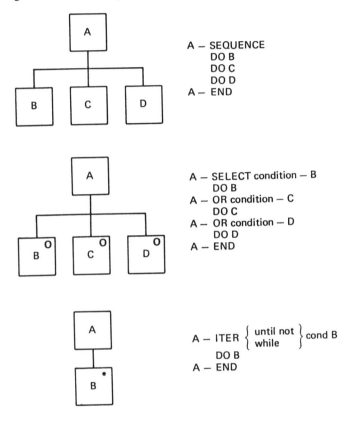

A — SEQUENCE
   DO B
   DO C
   DO D
A — END

A — SELECT condition — B
   DO B
A — OR condition — C
   DO C
A — OR condition — D
   DO D
A — END

A — ITER $\left\{ \begin{array}{l} \text{until not} \\ \text{while} \end{array} \right\}$ cond B
   DO B
A — END

*Figure 10.11*

```
A - SEQUENCE
    open FILE, REPORT
    read FILE record
    TOTAL = 0
    B1 - print title
    B2 - ITER until end of file (FILE)
        C - SEQUENCE
            D1 - ACCOUNT = 0
            store account number
            D2 - ITER until account number not = stored
            account number or end of file (FILE)
                F1 - SELECT credit record
                    G1 - ACCOUNT = ACCOUNT + CREDIT
                F1 - OR debit record
                    G2 - ACCOUNT = ACCOUNT - DEBIT
                F1 - END
                F2 - SEQUENCE
                    read FILE record
                    TOTAL = TOTAL + ACCOUNT
                F2 - END
            D2 - END
            D3 - print account line
        C - END
    B2 - END
    B3 - print total
    close FILE, REPORT
    stop
A - END
```

## Conclusion

In this chapter we have considered two contrasting methods for structured program design: Yourdon and Constantine's functional design and Jackson's data-oriented design. Functional design works from the techniques of DFDs and data dictionaries. Jackson's technique is less easy to place within a standard systems development methodology (although it must be said that Jackson has created his own). Clearly, to use JSP the analyst must have a clear idea of data structures. This suggests that techniques such as E – R diagramming and normalisation have a useful role in preparing for data-oriented program design (figure 10.12).

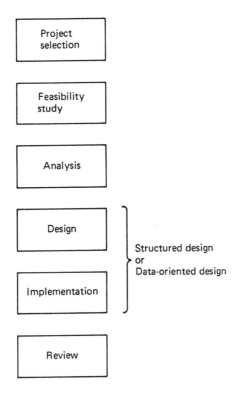

*Figure 10.12*

## Problems

1a. What is the main difference between a structure chart and a flowchart?
1b. What is the sequence of events in the following structure chart?

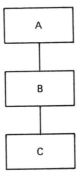

2. Create a structure chart from the DFD below.

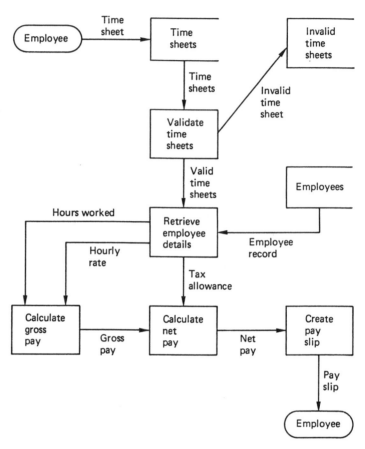

3. Compare ELH's and JSP. What do you think are the major similarities and differences between the two techniques?

# 11   Structured Walkthroughs

## Introduction

A structured walkthrough is a group review of any product of software development prior to its release into the project life cycle. It is also referred to as a peer group review, team debugging or ego-less programming.

Walkthroughs can take place at various stages in a project. During analysis, such items as E–R diagrams and DFDs might be subject to structured review. During the design phase, a walkthrough of structure charts might be considered. At the implementation phase, walkthroughs of programs and associated documentation are essential.

Credit for the structured walkthrough concept has been given to at least two different sources:

1. In his book *The Psychology of Computer Programming*, Weinberg (1971) suggested that one of the major problems with programming is that programmers see their programs too much as extensions of themselves. Since people have a natural tendency not to find fault with themselves, programmers are unable to detect errors in their programs satisfactorily. As a solution to this problem, Weiberg proposed that programming become 'ego-less' by allowing programs to be informally assessed by colleagues (Weinberg, 1971).
2. Team debugging is a technique developed by IBM as part of its chief programmer team approach to project organisation (see chapter 12). It was first employed on the *New York Times* project in the early 1970s (Baker, 1976).

## Why do we need structured walkthroughs?

Since the pioneering work by Weinberg and IBM, Edward Yourdon has probably been the most outspoken supporter of the validation of development products by teams of peers. Yourdon has maintained that structured walkthroughs have a number of tangible and intangible benefits for any organisation that uses them (Yourdon, 1978):

### Tangible benefits

1. Correctness. Organisations that subject all systems to stringent walk-throughs reportedly reduce the program error-rate from an average of three to five defects per hundred lines of program code to a more manageable average of three to five defects per thousand lines of code.
2. Standards. Walkthroughs are a useful way of establishing and enforcing standards for the analysis, design, coding, testing, and documentation of computer systems.
3. Readability. Walkthroughs improve the readability of programs and systems documentation, thereby aiding the maintenance process.

### Intangible benefits

1. Training. Walkthroughs have the effect of passing on good organisational practices to new company personnel.
2. Insurance. Walkthroughs disseminate information about systems throughout the organisation, thus offsetting the problems of high staff turnover.

### Group roles

A structured walkthrough is usually a group effort, with several people serving different roles within the team. A walkthrough team might consist, for example, of a presenter, a coordinator, a scribe, a maintenance critic, a standards critic, and one or more user representatives.

1. The presenter is usually the creator of the product to be reviewed. His or her role is to lead the team through an examination of this product.
2. The coordinator organises all the activities that occur or should occur prior to the walkthrough: for example, ascertaining that each team member has received a copy of the product to be reviewed prior to the walkthrough.
3. The scribe records the proceedings, and eventually forwards a report to management summarising the team's findings.
4. The maintenance critic inspects the product for any future maintenance problems.
5. The standards critic ascertains that the product adheres to organisational standards.
6. User representatives verify that the product performs as requested.

## Conduct of the walkthrough

Even though each team member has a primary role, all team members are equally accountable in terms of examining the quality of the system and offering comments and criticisms. The responsibility of the team is to give an accurate appraisal of the product being reviewed. All criticisms should be specific, indicating exactly where more work is needed. The participants should identify defects, but they should not attempt to correct them. Correction is the sole responsibility of the author or presenter.

During the walkthrough, participants are required to remain as objective as possible. In particular, they should especially remember to evaluate only the product itself, and not the person presenting it. A walkthrough can easily degenerate into heated and destructive argument if criticism becomes personal. Moreover, the participants should remember that in systems development there are many 'correct' solutions to a given problem. Participants should therefore not try to impose their own preferred solution to the problem under consideration.

The goal, however, is not to eliminate conflict entirely. Some studies have shown that objective disagreements can actually help to clarify issues, goals and requirements.

## Outcome of the walkthrough

The outcome of a walkthrough is the walkthrough report prepared by the scribe. This report comes in two parts: a summary, and an issues list.

On the summary, all participants must sign the report to show that they are in agreement with the decisions made. This enforces shared responsibility. At the bottom of the summary the final verdict is given. The product is accepted as it is with minor revisions or it is rejected. Rejection might be broken down into three categories:

1. The product has so many serious flaws that it must be completely rebuilt.
2. The product needs major revisions.
3. The review was incomplete and must continue later.

If the product is accepted subject to minor revisions, a second review is not required. Some member of the team is, however, assigned to see that the decisions made are carried out. If the product is rejected for whatever reason, at least one follow-up review is required.

The second page of the report, the issues list, details all the problems that need attention. As the problems are corrected, they are checked off this list by the team member assigned to monitor progress.

Managers are expected always to receive at least a copy of the summary. In contrast, the issues list is primarily for the benefit of the presenter. Figure 11.1 (a and b) details a sample walkthrough report.

```
                    WALKTHROUGH REPORT
                        SUMMARY

PRODUCT:  Edit Personnel Record Program   DATE: 2/3/88
PRESENTER:  P. Beynon-Davies              START: 10.30 am
                                          END: 11.00 am


COORDINATOR: Roger Coles
SCRIBE: Geoff Evans
OTHER PARTICIPANTS:
1. Phillip Davies
2. Gillian Roberts
3. Margaret Madeley
4.
5.


DECISION: Accepted with minor revisions required.
```

*Figure 11.1a*

```
                   WALKTHROUGH REPORT
                      ISSUES LIST

PRODUCT: Edit Personnel Record Program  DATE: 2/3/88
PRESENTER: P. Beynon-Davies
ISSUES REQUIRING ATTENTION:
1. Non-standard variable names.
2. Program does not allow for user override on screen edit.
```

*Figure 11.1b*

**Walkthrough as primary validation**

Walkthroughs are the primary validation mechanism in a structured development environment. Within each of the phases of the project life cycle, each major element of output from the stages will be subject to critical review. Hence, in the analysis phase, each diagram making up the requirements document will be subject to a walkthrough. Not only this, the finalised requirement document as a whole will be subject to some form of review to ensure that it forms a consistent package. Figure 11.2 details the place of structured walkthroughs within the model of systems development discussed in chapter 1.

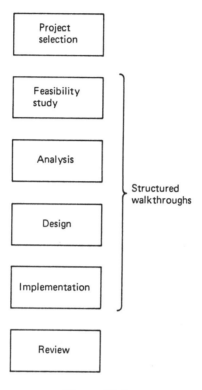

*Figure 11.2*

## Summary

1. A structured walkthrough is a peer group review of any product of software development.
2. Each member of a walkthrough team is assigned at least one role, namely as presenter, coordinator, scribe, maintenance critic, standards critic or user representative.
3. All team members are accountable for the quality of the product examined.
4. All criticism in a walkthrough should be constructive and specific. No criticism should be destructive, personal or unspecific.
5. The end-result of a walkthrough is the walkthrough report made up of a summary and an issues list.

# 12   Integrated Project Support Environments

## Introduction

An integrated project support environment (IPSE for short) aims to provide a total working environment for the professional software engineer. An IPSE is one example of CASE (computer-aided software engineering) – a topic currently receiving much attention in the computing literature.

The motivation for developing IPSEs arose on two fronts. First, from some pioneering work done at IBM on the composition of programming teams for large-scale projects (Baker, 1972). Second, from the difficulty of supporting such large-scale software engineering projects with the facilities provided by conventional operating systems and stand-alone tools (Kernighan and Plauger, 1976).

For example, the information manipulated by conventional tools is usually stored as files on some medium. It is rare for information to be kept concerning the relationships between such files. This means that requirements and design specifications frequently do not reflect changes made in the implementation of a piece of software, which can lead to problems in software maintenance.

Also, in large-scale developments, such files tend to be shared between different members of a project team. When changes are made to the products of the development process, such changes should be distributed to all affected members of the team. This problem of change control is extremely difficult to manage using conventional tools.

IPSEs are intended to address the problems outlined above by providing a set of tools covering the whole of the project life cycle, and supporting many different roles in the development process in one coherent framework.

## A development model

The IPSE or CASE concept works with a particular model of the software development process. In this model, the development process is seen as being represented by a set of activities operating on objects to produce other objects. The objects manipulated by such activities will often be documents, diagrams or even programs. However, they may be more abstractly thought of as elements in the analysis, design and implementation of an information system. Similarly, the activities involved may be relatively formal (for example, compile a program or carry out a test) or informal (for example, obtain user's requirements, etc.).

The stages of structured analysis and design are made up of a number of activities. These activities involve the production of diagrams used to document the workings either of existing systems, or of proposed systems. These are the objects of the development process discussed above. An IPSE provides facilities for such objects to be created, manipulated and communicated between members of a project team.

## Gearing

In other words, the facilities provided by an IPSE act to improve the effectiveness of a company in producing information systems. It can do this by providing a gearing effect at three different levels (Snowdon et al, 1985):

1. Individual
2. Project
3. Corporate

### *Individual gearing*

Individual activities within the development model will be carried out solely by one agent. In many cases the agent will be a person, but in some cases it may involve a number of people engaged in the same activity. The individual gearing that can be provided by an IPSE is concerned with enabling an agent to carry out its activities more effectively. Measures of effectiveness might include both time and accuracy.

Examples of the types of facilities included in an IPSE to facilitate individual gearing include:

1. For a programmer
   – better compilers (e.g. faster, better diagnostics)
   – newer languages (e.g. 4GLs)
   – newer methods, encouraging better implementation (e.g. data structure diagrams)
2. For an analyst
   – better analysis and design facilities (e.g. diagramming tools)
3. For a project manager
   – control tools, PERTs, spreadsheets etc.

### Project gearing

A project may be considered as a coordinated set of activities involving a number of individuals, each contributing to the overall aims of the project. Whereas IPSE support for individual roles concentrates on gearing the activities relating to these specific roles, IPSE support at the project level is concerned with providing means by which the set of activities comprising the project as a whole are made more effective.

The sort of support that an IPSE can include at this level are:

1. Integration and cohesion of tools and information representation to provide smooth ways in which information can flow among individuals within a project.
2. Support for project standards. The system should encourage rather than enforce the observation of standards by incorporating their features within the IPSEs facilities.
3. Maintenance of automatic version control.
4. Allowing the project manager to keep control over the ongoing state of the project using tools which monitor progress.

### Corporate gearing

Both individual and project gearing are secondary to the major objective of making the business more effective. In any business reliant on information systems, there will be a number of separate, but interrelated, projects. The effectiveness of the company in carrying out these projects will depend, for example, upon its ability to control the interrelationships and cross-dependencies amongst them. Such relationships might be technical (for example, one project relies on the results of another), to do with resourcing (for example, one project may rely on another project finishing to release key skills) or concerned with business achievement and finance.

Examples of facilities which relate to gearing at the corporate level include:

1. Control of inter-project relationships.
2. Construction and utilisation of a corporate 'experience-base' – for example, the availability of a corporate component library, together with the means of developing subsequent systems using this library.
3. Dissemination of standard working practices, methods, and tools which are tailored to the business needs of the company.

### The information systems factory

Part of the now-extinct Alvey programme devoted its attention to the goals of improving quality and productivity in software engineering. To help achieve this, attention focused on the concept of an information systems factory (ISF), which is a facility enabling the effective production of future information systems.

The Alvey software engineering strategy envisaged the development of three generations of IPSE as a means of attaining the ISF.

1. IPSE 1 is broadly the environment provided by present-day UNIX, utilising its tools and filing structure.
2. IPSE 2 is seen as employing database technology, rather than the elementary file-store, to solve the problem of providing distributed access to the support system (BIS/IPSE).
3. IPSE 3 is expected to make considerable inroads into methods developed from knowledge based systems (chapter 14), as well as provide support for advanced capabilities involved in the work on formal methods (chapter 18).

### The BIS/IPSE

The DFD in figure 12.1 describes the IPSE produced by BIS Applied Systems. This IPSE supports the project life cycle in three major ways. First, it offers a range of facilities, centring around the production of system documentation, which aid the information systems development process (process 2). Second, it may be used to manage these sets of system documentation (process 3). Third, it provides a number of facilities which aid the process of managing projects (process 4).

These three functions operate by reference to a standards library which can be tailored to suit the requirements of a particular installation (process 5). In addition, control of the machine itself is performed through the system administration function (process 1).

Let us take a more detailed look at each of these processes in turn.

### *System administration*

The BIS/IPSE distinguishes between users of the system in terms of 'sign-on roles'. This means that the user.IDs acceptable to the system are categorised according to the various roles which users of the system may have. Nine different types of user are distinguished:

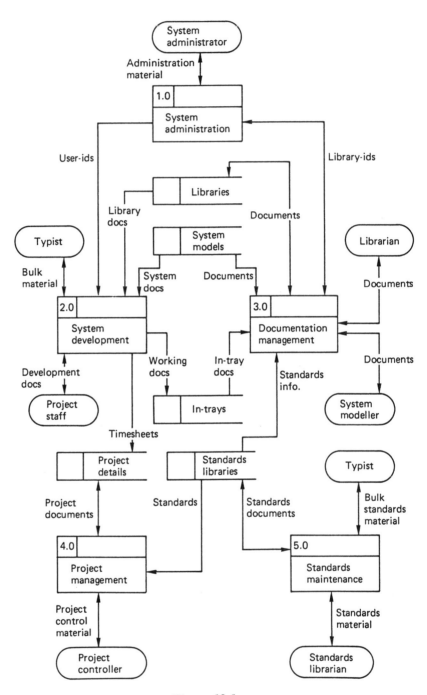

*Figure 12.1*

1. System administrator.
2. Project staff.
3. Librarian.
4. System modeller.
5. Projects administrator.
6. Project controller.
7. Typist.
8. Standards librarian.
9. Back-up administrator.

Most users are categorised as either project staff or typists. The other roles are used as required. For instance, the system administration function is responsible for the smooth running of the installation. It involves:

1. Powering up and powering down the machine.
2. Control of access to the system facilities through user and library IDs.
3. Maintaining security copies of file systems.
4. Monitoring of disk space utilisation.
5. Control of print-spoolers.
6. Control of remote job-entry facilities.

## System development

The system development facilities are designed mainly for use by project staff. They are primarily designed to aid the production of documentation needed within system development. Such documentation may consist of both text and diagrams: text in the form of project reports, process descriptions etc., and diagrams in the form of DFDs E–R diagrams, etc. A subset of the facilities can be used by typists to enter documentation in bulk.

This is in many ways the heart of the IPSE. It is clearly designed to service the needs of computing professionals working within some sort of development framework such as SSADM.

## Documentation management

During its production, documentation resides in work-areas which are owned by individual users of the system. To make an item of documentation generally available it must be moved to an in-tray associated with a documentation library or system model. A system model is a cross-referenced set of documents used to describe the various components of a given application system. A documentation library is a set of documents used to support the development of a particular application.

Each documentation library is made the responsibility of an individual known as a librarian. Each system model is made the responsibility of the system modeller. Documentation management facilities are used by librarians and system modellers to process the individual in-trays making up project development.

Documents held in a library or system model may only be changed by taking a copy of the document into an individual work area, amending the document, and then moving it into the appropriate in-tray.

### Project management

The IPSE's project management facilities enable the structure of a project to be defined in terms of phases, tasks and sub-tasks. Phases are defined as groups of logically related tasks leading to a defined checkpoint. Tasks are major units of work to be performed within each phase. Sub-tasks are the detailed units of work to be performed within each task.

Estimates of time needed can be recorded at each of these levels in terms of start dates, end dates, man-days/hours, and man-day costs. Actual assignment of work to individuals is, however, performed only at the level of sub-tasks. Actual time spent on sub-tasks is captured by means of on-line time-sheets which are filled in by individual users.

A number of reports can be automatically produced from this information. For example:

1. Phase completion dates. This report provides a summary of authorised and currently estimated completion dates, and the difference between them, in terms of phases. Authorised completion dates are those initially assigned to a project. Currently estimated completion dates are 're-estimates' of time to go using information captured from timesheets.
2. Project breakdowns. Project breakdowns analyse project costs and days spent by phase within project. Costs are derived from charge-rates assigned to each individual making up a project team.
3. Phase breakdowns. Phase breakdowns detail authorised estimates of days' effort, time spent, time estimated to complete, and estimated completion dates by assignment within phase.

### Standards maintenance

System development and documentation management are performed by reference to a standards library. This standards library may contain, among other things, on-line standards manuals, document skeletons, and some indication of conventions to be employed in systems development.

The standards library may be defined separately for each installation and is maintained by the standards librarian. Facilities are however provided for typists to key-in bulk documents to be included in the standards library.

## Conclusion

The first generation of CASE tools, such as those categorised under Alvey's IPSE 1 idea, provided the means for improving programmer productivity. Thus, one often hears references to a subset of the UNIX environment as being 'the programmer's workbench' (Kernighan, 1976). The second generation of CASE tools, an example of which is the BIS/IPSE, have attempted to improve the productivity of the systems analyst. In other words, the contemporary emphasis is on providing a bundle of tools which we might collectively call 'the analyst's workbench'.

Although we have used the term 'workbench' in both of these contexts, the workbench concept should not be characterised with meanings such as 'individual' or 'alone'. One of the major emphases, particularly of tools like the BIS/IPSE is to encourage support for teams of personnel making up a project or projects.

Productivity is undoubtedly the large issue defined by this endeavour. There are, however, a number of smaller issues which need to be addressed. Automation of many aspects of the system development process has been shown to produce better systems in the sense of encouraging standards and facilitating greater communication between the user and the analyst. There are, though, a number of problems at least with the present generation of IPSE. For instance, most IPSEs are relatively expensive packages that demand changes in work patterns. Also, most IPSEs work within a particular methodological framework. To use the IPSE effectively the analyst needs to understand and work within this framework. This means that an organisation should not be encouraged to invest in this technology without a thorough analysis of its framework for systems development. IPSEs are production tools, not a panacea for all software ailments.

# 13   Fourth-generation Environments

## Introduction

Third-generation languages such as COBOL, Pascal and FORTRAN are inherently procedural in nature. That is, the programmer is required to specify not only 'what' is needed, but also 'how' the computer is expected to solve the problem in a detailed step-by-step manner. In contrast, fourth-generation languages (4GLs) are designed to be largely non-procedural. The programmer need only specify 'what' is required, and leave the 'how' to the 4GL to sort out. Another way of expressing this is to say that any algorithm is made up of two components: logic and control (Kowalski, 1979). In a third-generation language (3GL), logic and control are necessarily intertwined. The programmer expresses both the solution to the problem and such things as sequencing and iteration in one medium. In a 4GL some indication of the logic of the system is given: of the general structure of the data needed to support a system, the general format of the output needed from the system, and the form of the interface needed between the user and the system. No indication is given, at least in the 4GL, of the control needed to accomplish the processing.

## Components of a 4GL

The range of products which can be conveniently collected under the umbrella-term of a 4GL includes:

1. Data dictionary: a place for storing the specifications both of the data used, and of the databases where this data is physically located.
2. Screen painter: used to outline the format of any on-line displays needed by the system.
3. Report generator: used to specify print-out formats, normally by reference to the database structures stored in the data dictionary.
4. Query language: a means of flexibly specifying non-procedural queries on a database.
5. Dialogue specifier: used to indicate the nature of program flow, where this is not apparent from the non-procedural information supplied.

138

6. Code generator: a means of connecting up with traditional 3GL systems by generating COBOL code from data dictionary definitions.

## The application generator

An application generator is a more comprehensive term for most of the elements discussed above. Application generators are designed to create one or more 'standard' types of application such as data entry screens, enquiry programs, menus, reports, forms and batch programs. They work typically by displaying a series of screens on which a series of parameters are specified. These parameters are then either interpreted when the application is run, or are compiled into some form of source code.

In the case of an update program, for example, the programmer would specify which files are to be updated from the program, the fields from those files to be displayed on the screen for editing, and the restrictions to be placed on the information to be entered. The application could then be run without further input from the programmer.

This approach works well when the data are not too complex. It is insufficient however for more complex applications required by most DP departments. One approach to solving this problem is to offer more screens so that the programmer can enter parameters specifying the application in greater detail. Clearly however, this approach is limited by the fact that the parameter screens can become so complex as to be unusable. The answer adopted by most products is therefore to generalise as many of the user requirements as possible by using the non-procedural approach, but then to offer 'hooks' where the programmer can attach modules of traditional 3GL code.

## 4GLs, data dictionaries, and relational databases

Many 4GLs are designed to be used in association with a data dictionary and/or a relational database. Both of these technologies possess characteristics that help speed up the application development process. The dictionary, for instance, acts as a single source for all the data needed during the development process. The tabular nature of relational databases simplifies much of the processing needed to be performed by any program.

Many people consider 4GLs to be one of the central components of a fourth-generation applications environment. Along with relational databases, integrated project support environments and structured systems analysis and design methodologies also connect well with 4GLs. This is because 4GLs, RDBMSs, IPSEs and SSADM all work around the concept of some form of central repository of meta data, that is, data about data. The various forms of such data are all encapsulated under one inclusive term – that of a data dictionary.

## Data dictionary systems

In chapter 7 we considered the use of logical data dictionaries in the analysis and design of information systems. In this section we consider how a piece of software, called a data dictionary system (DDS), is being increasingly used as a data administration and production tool.

Whereas a logical data dictionary records details about information requirements in conceptual terms, a physical data dictionary gives information about data processing applications in computing terms. The processes of the logical data model are therefore described as systems, programs and program-modules in the physical data model. The data (flows, stores, entities and relationships) are described in terms of databases, files, records and fields.

## The elements of a physical model

In the physical model of an information system there will be a number of elements describing processes and data. Each such element might be described in various ways. For example, data elements might need to be described in terms of:

1. The names associated with an element. Different names may be used by various users and computer programs to refer to one element.
2. A description of the data element in natural language.
3. Details of ownership – normally the department that creates the data.
4. Details of the users who refer to the element.
5. Details of the systems and programs that refer to or update the element.
6. The security level attached to the element in order to restrict access.
7. Physical details about the element: length of the data item, type of data item (numeric, alphanumeric, etc.).
8. The validation rules for each data element.
9. Details of the relationship of the data item to other data items.
10. Logical details about the element: which logical entities contain the data element.

**Facilities of a data dictionary system**

A data dictionary often forms a database under the control of the enterprise DBMS just like all the other databases of interest to the organisation. The team of data dictionary and DBMS we might call a data dictionary system, since the DBMS provides facilities for maintaining the data dictionary, producing reports from it, and so on. As well as standard DBMS functions however, a more sophisticated DBMS might have the following facilities (BCS, 1976):

1. Automatic input from source code of data definitions.
2. The ability to handle several versions of the same program or data structure at the same time.
3. The provision of facilities to generate application programs.

One of the main functions of a data dictionary system should be to show the relationship between the conceptual and implementation views, and identify any inconsistencies between the two (Avison, 1985). No presently available DDS performs this function, but some of the facilities discussed in chapter 12 are beginning to move in this direction.

**Advantages of using a data dictionary system**

A data dictionary system can be conceived of as probably the central support component for any modern development methodology. A DDS is a core component of IPSEs, 4GLs and RDBMSs. This is because a number of benefits arise from using a DDS:

1. Improved ability of management to control and know about the data resources of the enterprise.
2. Reduced clerical workload involved in administering the databases of the enterprise.
3. System development is aided by providing facilities for documenting information collected during all stages of the project life-cycle.
4. System maintenance is aided, in that any changes to data structures can be consistently applied at one time to all affected systems.
5. System analysts and programmers are encouraged to follow structured methodologies.

## Oracle

As an example of something approaching what we mean by a fourth-generation environment we present here a description of ORACLE, a relational database management system and applications development tool available from the Oracle Corporation of California.

ORACLE uses Structured Query Language, SQL for short, for all its data management operations. SQL is thus much more than just a query language. SQL has become the standard non-procedural interface to relational databases, and as such contains facilities for:

1. File maintenance: creating and deleting tables; inserting, amending and deleting records.
2. Information retrieval: queries and reports.
3. Privacy and security: granting and revoking access; creating and removing views.

## Sample SQL commands

Suppose that we have a company requirement to produce the database of information shown in figure 13.1. The structure for each of the tables in the database can be set up using the create command, as for the sales table:

```
CREATE TABLE SALES
     (Sales_no char(4) NOT NULL,
      Product_no char(4),
      Customer_no char(4),
      Qty number(3))
```

The 'CREATE' statement allows us to specify a name for a table, and the names, data types and lengths of each of the attributes in the table. There is, however, no direct mechanism in SQL for specifying the primary key of a table.

```
Salesforce
----------
```

| Salesman-no | Salesman-name | Sales-area | Sales-target |
|---|---|---|---|
| 01 | Jones S | Cardiff | 2,000 |
| 03 | Jenkins P | Valleys | 1,500 |
| 02 | Thomas J | Newport | 1,700 |
| 04 | Davies A | Swansea | 600 |

Customers
---------

| Customer-no | Customer-name | Sales-area |
|---|---|---|
| 01 | Friendly Foods | Cardiff |
| 03 | Rookem Insurance | Newport |
| 02 | Dodgy Videos | Valleys |
| 04 | Custom Cars | Swansea |
| 06 | Raunchy Restaurants | Valleys |

Sales
-----

| Sales-no | Product-no | Customer-no | Qty |
|---|---|---|---|
| 1004 | 014 | 03 | 20 |
| 2053 | 014 | 02 | 40 |
| 1342 | 028 | 04 | 30 |
| 1556 | 028 | 06 | 50 |
| 2555 | 014 | 06 | 30 |

Products
--------

| Product-no | Product-description | Supplier-no |
|---|---|---|
| 014 | Wonderful Widget | 1432 |
| 032 | Sticky Stationery | 2468 |
| 028 | Stampy Stapler | 3521 |
| 056 | Bandy Binder | 2468 |

Stock
-----

| Product-no | Qty-in-Stock | Re-order Level |
|---|---|---|
| 014 | 200 | 30 |
| 032 | 300 | 50 |
| 028 | 250 | 40 |

```
Suppliers
---------


Supplier-no      Supplier-name        Sup-address      Sup-tel

1432             Widgets Inc.         Crosby           246832
2468             Standard Stationery  Leeds            438127
3521             Standard Staplers    London           381766
```

*Figure 13.1*

If we recall the discussion in chapter 3 on relational database systems, a primary key is defined as an attribute whose values are first, unique, and second, not null. If either of these characteristics is violated, it then becomes impossible to use such an attribute to identify a row in a table.

SQL does allow us to specify each of these characteristics for an attribute independently. First, we can specify any attribute of a table as being NOT NULL, as in the case of sales_no above. This forces users always to provide a value for this attribute when inserting data into a table. Second, we can declare a unique index for any attribute of a table. Thus, in the example below, we set up a unique index with the filename sales.ind on the sales number attribute of the sales table:

```
CREATE UNIQUE INDEX sales.ind ON sales(sales_no)
```

Having set up the tables in the manner described above, we can enter information into the tables using the insert command:

```
INSERT INTO Customers
VALUES (01,'Friendly Foods','Cardiff')
```

We can also maintain the database through use of the update and delete comands as below:

```
UPDATE Customers
SET Sales_area = 'Valleys'
WHERE Customer_no = 01
------------------------
DELETE FROM Customers
WHERE Customer_no = 01
```

SQL was however, designed, primarily as a means for extracting data from a database. Such extraction is accomplished through use of the select command: a combination of the select, project and join operators of relational algebra as described in chapter 3. For instance, the select statement below extracts data from the salesforce and customers tables of relevance to salesman working in the Valleys sales area, and orders it by the salesman_no attribute. Note the way in which information is joined across two tables by indicating the common attribute in the WHERE clause:

```
SELECT salesman_no, salesman_name, customer_no, customer_name
FROM salesforce, customers
WHERE salesforce.sales_area = customers.sales_area
 AND  customers.sales_area = 'Valleys'
ORDER BY salesman_no
```

Complex queries can be written in SQL to produce paginated reports. The example below will produce a report of total sales by sales area and product number:

```
COLUMN Sales-area HEADING 'SALES:AREA'
COLUMN Product-no HEADING 'PRODUCT:NO'
COLUMN Qty HEADING 'SALES'
BREAK ON Sales-area, Product-no
COMPUTE SUM OF Qty ON Sales-area
TITLE 'SALES BY SALES-AREA'
SELECT Sales-area, Product-no, Qty
FROM CUSTOMERS, SALES
WHERE CUSTOMERS.Customer-no = SALES.Customer-no
ORDER BY Sales-area, Product-no
```

The primary mechanism for enforcing integrity issues in SQL is through the concept of a view, discussed briefly in chapter 3 . Views are virtual tables which act as 'windows' on the database composed of real tables. The view below establishes a virtual table for use by a salesman working in the Valleys sales area. Such a salesman granted access only to this view would be unable to see information of relevance to other sales areas in the company's sales profile.

```
CREATE VIEW VALLEYS
AS SELECT Customer_no, Customer_name, Sales_no, Product_no, Qty
   FROM Sales, Customers
   WHERE Sales.Customer_no = Customers.Customer_no
     AND Sales_area = 'Valleys'
```

**Application development**

An interactive environment is available for application development under ORACLE consisting of a number of tools:

SQL*PLUS: an extended version of SQL as described above.

SQL*REPORT: a report writing module.

SQL*FORMS: a screen painter for producing data entry screens and displays.

SQL*MENUS: a facility for packaging reports and forms together.

SQL*DD: an on-line data dictionary, available to aid in developing ORACLE applications.

**Conclusion**

The primary benefit of a 4GL for the computer professional is that standard applications can be developed easily and quickly. A typical small application system written in COBOL might take somewhere in the region of 12 man-days. The same system written in a 4GL is likely to take about 3-6 hours.

4GLs also have the advantage of producing relatively bug-free maintainable applications with a consistent user interface. Applications can therefore be developed incrementally at reasonable cost to the organisation. We shall discuss this in more detail when we come to consider the prototyping approach to systems development (chapter 16).

# 14  Knowledge-based Systems

## Introduction

Knowledge-based systems (KBS) have recently been much discussed in the computing literature. They have been widely heralded as the next generation in software technology. This chapter attempts to explain exactly what is meant by a KBS and make some suggestions as to its place within future software development.

The easiest way to approach the problem of defining a KBS is by contrast with what is presently available, namely database systems. More particularly, many people believe that one type of database model offers the most fruitful foundation on which to build. This is the relational database model, as discussed in chapter 3.

## Information and knowledge

Standard relational databases store facts about the entities or objects in some domain, and some primitive information about the relationships between such entities or objects. For instance, in the sales example described in chapter 3, the database represents two entities, namely a Salesman and a Customer. A Salesman is related to a Customer in the following way: only one Salesman services one Sales_area, but each Sales_area encompasses a number of Customers. Such a relationship is said to be a one-to-many relationship: one Salesman to many Customers. We can draw an E–R diagram to represent this relationship (see chapter 5).

Facts can thus be thought of either as classifications of entities, or as detailing relationships between entities. For example, Peter, John, Ann and Fred can be thought of as entities. They can be assigned to the class Person. Similarly, we can define relationships between entities. For instance, John and Peter may be involved in the management relationship – John manages Peter.

Traditional relational databases represent such relationships by values stored in tables. Hence, in a table of employee records we might have a field detailing the personnel number of an immediate superior. Databases

147

are however particularly ineffective at representing other aspects of knowledge of interest to people in the real world, namely rules.

Rules are important because they enable us to specify how to infer new instances of a class of entities, or new instances of a relationship, from hitherto unclassified entities. For example, suppose we have the following rule which applies to our enterprise.

IF A manages B
   AND B manages C
THEN C reports-to A

This simple rule allows us to deduce the fact that Fred reports-to John from the following facts:

Peter manages John
John manages Ann
Ann manages Fred

In other words:

IF John manages Ann
   AND Ann manages Fred
THEN Fred reports-to John

## Declarative and procedural knowledge

Speaking abstractly then, knowledge can be said to consist of both facts and rules. Facts are often referred to as declarative knowledge, whereas rules are often referred to as procedural knowledge.

Facts are well-represented in traditional relational databases. Rules can also be represented, in a fashion. For instance, the 'reports-to' rule above can be represented by storing values in another table which records the reporting relationship. Doing this for each such rule in our organisation will, however, soon cause an 'information explosion'. We would need tables to represent all possible associations between entities, and this is clearly not feasible.

This highlights the primary role of rules. They are really mechanisms for managing the 'information explosion' possibilities inherent in any attempt to represent aspects of the real world. They are a more concise way of representing reality. In our example above therefore, it is probably more practical to represent such rules as the 'reports-to' function by some hard-code in an application system.

It is useful therefore to make the distinction between procedural and declarative knowledge and a procedural and declarative representation for such knowledge. Procedural knowledge is traditionally represented in a procedural manner as high-level language code. What KBSs are attempting to do however is in a sense to treat procedural knowledge, like the 'reports-to' function, as stored data; that is, to store it in a declarative representation. This knowledge will then be activated by a separate general-purpose processor which will perform all the appropriate inferencing in any particular case.

## Representing knowledge declaratively

The major advantage of representing knowledge declaratively in this manner is that it makes for easier maintenance. Adding a rule to a knowledge base is a relatively simple matter. Incorporating an additional rule into a section of 3GL code is not an easy task; it normally involves modifying the whole program.

The process of modifying a rule in a knowledge base is also straight-forward. It involves either adding or deleting a condition (IF part), or adding or deleting a conclusion (THEN part). Modifying the processing of a traditional program is a very different matter.

In a sense, the attempts made to design traditional commercial systems as a set of independent but interacting modules (as described in chapter 10) are an attempt to emulate many of the features of the declarative approach that we have been discussing (Yourdon, 1978). The modular design of systems is an attempt to handle functionality in procedure-like chunks which emulate rules in our knowledge base.

Representing knowledge declaratively enables knowledge to be in some sense modular or independent of the process that uses it. Moving on from our discussion of relational database management systems, we might call this an example of knowledge–process independence. Figures 14.1 and 14.2 represent two different ways of representing the processing involved in cashing a cheque at a bank, one procedural, the other declarative.

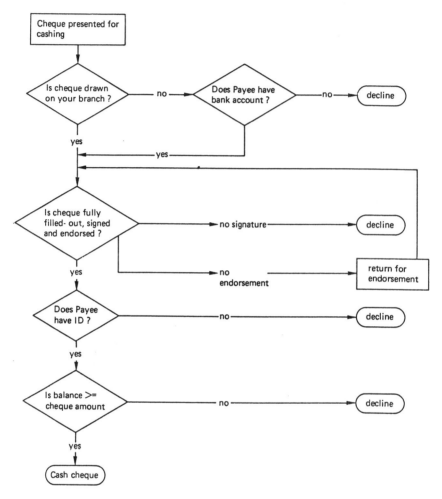

*Figure 14.1 A procedural representation for banking knowledge*

## Inference

In a KBS therefore, facts and rules are represented in a declarative manner, that is, as data. This leads us to the other important architectural difference between a KBS and a conventional system: the separation of inference and knowledge.

```
1. IF cheque is complete
      AND payee is known
      AND funds are covered
   THEN cash cheque

2. IF cheque is correctly dated
      AND cheque is signed by originator
      AND amount match
      AND payee is identified
      AND cheque is endorsed by payee
   THEN cheque is complete

3. IF date on cheque is todays date
      OR a date from 1 to 90 days prior
         to today's date
   THEN cheque is dated correctly
```

*Figure 14.2 A declarative representation for banking knowledge*

The word inference is derived from the Latin words *in* and *ferre*, meaning 'to carry or bring'. Inference is therefore the process of bringing or carrying forward old knowledge into new knowledge. In our example above, the old knowledge represented by our collection of facts is turned into new knowledge, a new fact, by the application of inference; in our case the application of a rule.

Every computer system has an inferencing capability or inference 'engine'. In a conventional system, written say in a procedural language such as COBOL, the inference engine is represented by those parts of the program code that control the processing of the system. A conventional program or system has a limited inference capability that is totally intertwined with the knowledge it has to process. In our banking example, for instance, the procedural representation specifies in great detail the logic to be followed in cashing a cheque.

In a KBS, the knowledge is separated out from the inferencing mechanism. The inference engine in a KBS is therefore a program which accesses not only data as in a conventional system, but also pieces of procedural knowledge as well. In our declarative representation, the logic is therefore implicit rather than explicit. We detail the rules for cashing a cheque, but leave it to the inference engine to control or execute the process of encashment.

In many ways this separation of inference and knowledge makes the process of system development that much easier. In developing a conventional system, the software engineer has to detail both the 'what' and the 'how': what the system is required to do, and how it is expected to do it. The development of a KBS moves closer to the ideal of requiring the developer simply to specify the 'what', that is, to declare what rules and facts are needed in the system. The question of how this knowledge is to be made to work, or inferenced, can largely be ignored.

## Expert database systems

The eventual aim of a KBS is probably to represent all knowledge in one way. Many people, for instance, feel that the right direction is to represent declarative and procedural knowledge in the form of some notation based on the predicate calculus – a form of logic. As a stepping-stone in the direction of a full KBS however, another approach is to consider the interaction of two pieces of existing software: a DBMS and an expert system. The DBMS supports the conventional information processing; the expert system supports the rule-based processing.

## Expert systems and expert system shells

Many definitions of the term 'expert system' are available. The one used here is provided by Alex Goodall in his book *The Guide to Expert Systems* (Goodall, 1986).

> 'An expert system is a computer system that uses a representation of human expertise in a particular domain in order to perform functions similar to those normally performed by a human expert in that domain.'

Most of the early and classic expert systems such as MYCIN (Shortliffe, 1976) were built up incrementally over long periods of time using a language such as LISP. The knowledge in such a system was therefore 'hard-wired', as a large chunk of LISP code.

As the knowledge engineering discipline developed it became evident that new expert systems need not be built from scratch in the manner described above, but that they could borrow a great deal from previously built systems. The way to do this was to separate out the domain-specific knowledge in the expert system from that part which drives the system or does the 'thinking'. The former entity is now usually referred to as the knowledge base, and the latter as the inference engine.

This strategy has resulted in a new category of software tool for knowledge engineering – the expert system shell. A shell is an expert system without the domain specific knowledge. At its most basic it is made up of two elements: an inferencing mechanism, and a means for constructing a knowledge base.

**An example expert system shell**

To give readers a flavour of what we mean by this important interaction, let us first detail the characteristics of a typical expert system shell. Our expert system shell is designed primarily around the production rule formalism. This means that knowledge is coded into the system in terms of rules of the form:

```
if  identifier  is  value
    and  identifier  is  value
           ...
then  identifier  is  value
    and  identifier  is  value
           ...
```

For example, in an expert system for advising on whether or not a bank should give credit to its customers we might find the rule:

```
if customer_status is house_owner
    and customer_salary is sufficient
then credit_rating is good
```

The default inference mechanism in our shell employs what is called backward chaining. This means that to run the system, the user normally selects a query from an initial menu. This query is then set up as the goal for the system to solve. It does this by searching through the knowledge base for a rule which has an identifier in its THEN part that matches the identifier in the goal. For instance, if the current query is credit_rating, the rule above would be activated, meaning that two further sub-goals would be set up for customer_status and customer_salary. The value of customer_status might then be requested of the user by a question set in the system. In contrast, the value of customer_salary might be set by firing a further rule in the system:

```
if customer_net_monthly_salary  >  3 * monthly_repayment
then customer_salary is sufficient
```

This would mean that the inference engine would now try to find a value for customer_net_monthly_salary.

Backward chaining is often described as goal-directed, since reasoning moves back from the goal to initial data. In contrast, our shell also supports forward chaining, so-called because the reasoning process is directed by the data available to the final goal. Here the user directs the inference process by writing explicit control into the knowledge base. One way of doing this is by means of 'demons', that is, rules beginning with WHEN rather than IF. These are triggered as soon as the condition which they test becomes true. For example:

```
when customer_status is bankrupt
then report credit is impossible
```

The most straightforward way of implementing forward chaining is, however, through the use of meta rules. These look like low-level rules except that they explicitly detail the procedure to be followed. For example:

```
if query analysis
then check general information
    and check details
    and check advice
        . . . .
```

### Connecting the knowledge base to the database

Many of the early expert systems such as MYCIN (Shortliffe, 1976), R1 (McDermott, 1980) and PROSPECTOR (Gaschnig, 1982) were originally constructed to solve problems in domains substantially removed from mainstream commercial data processing. One effect of this has been to direct DP professionals to consider and develop applications in their own areas which are heavily inspired by the much publicised work in areas such as medical diagnosis (Reitman, 1984; Winston and Prendergast, 1984). This has meant that expert system applications in commerce have been seen from a restricted view point: that of the standalone system used for diagnostics, advice or some other popular category emphasised in the historical development of expert systems (Debenham, 1988).

At present, expert systems and conventional information systems constitute 'islands' of computing with little or no connection to each other. It is the purpose of this chapter to portray briefly developments which may act as bridges between these islands (Silverman, 1987). The thesis of this chapter is that a high proportion of commercial data processing, including all non-trivial database applications, would benefit from the application of expert systems.

## What is an expert database system

Traditionally, expert systems have been built with little or no connection to conventional databases. Hence, their primary mode of working has been continually to prompt the user for the information needed to arrive at a particular conclusion. This we might call stand-alone mode. Recently however, research has been directed towards investigating the important interaction between a knowledge base and a database. This mode, which we might call database mode, is the subject of this chapter.

An expert database system is one example architecture for a commercially useful KBS. This form of KBS is made up of two components: an expert system and a database management system or DBMS. The expert system is used to run the knowledge base; the DBMS is used to run the database. The intention is for the two to interact with each other to produce some 'intelligent' behaviour (Kerschberg, 1987a,)

## Types of expert database system

There are a variety of ways in which an expert system might interact with a database. For the purposes of discussion we shall roughly distinguish between three types of expert database system (EDS) (Al-Zobaidie and Grimson, 1987).

1. An enhanced database system
2. An enhanced expert system
3. Interdependent expert system and database.

### *Enhanced database system*

In this type of EDS, a deductive component is joined with the DBMS, thus producing an enhanced database system. There are three possible ways of linking this deductive component to a DBMS (Jarke and Vassilion, 1984).

1. Embedding. Deductive routines are embedded within the DBMS itself, and act as one more facility of the DBMS.
2. Filtering. User and application program queries are directed through a deductive component before being processed by the DBMS. In this sense, the deductive component acts as an interface between the DBMS and the user or application programs.
3. Interaction. The DBMS, rather than user or application programs, interacts with the deductive component.

The general idea behind linking a deductive component to a DBMS in one of these three ways is to improve either the efficiency or the functionality of the DBMS. Increased efficiency can result from techniques such as query optimisation, which have proved effective for instance in the whole area of relational database systems. Increased functionality can be demonstrated by supporting such elements as natural language interfaces, multiple user views, integrity constraints and mechanisms for handling incomplete data within the DBMS environment (Stonebraker and Rowe, 1985).

### Enhanced expert system

An enhanced database system involves the enhancement of a DBMS with some 'intelligent' software. In contrast, the second type of EDS involves enhancement to an expert system by extending its data management facilities (Jarke and Vassilion, 1984). This can be done in one of two ways:

- Internal enhancement. These systems extend the programming language in which the expert system is written (for example, PROLOG). This in effect gives the expert system its own internal DBMS (Walker, 1984).
- External enhancement. Probably of more interest to commercial data processing is the type of EDS which has been enhanced with external links. That is, the inference engine of the expert system is provided with direct access to a general-purpose, external DBMS. This allows the EDS to be tightly or loosely coupled to the database. In a loosely coupled system there is no dynamic link between the expert system and the database. Data is usually down-loaded to the expert system from the database as a 'snapshot' prior to the execution of the expert system. In a tightly coupled system, data is retrieved from the database only when required during the execution of the expert system. The DBMS however, still acts in the capacity of a slave to the expert system.

### Interdependent expert system and database

The first two types of EDS involve the enhancement of either the expert system or the database with the facilities available to the other. The third type of EDS that we wish to discuss allows the expert system and database to exist as independent systems that communicate down a common data channel. This permits the expert system and DBMS to operate either as two entirely separate systems with their own set of users, or as two cooperating systems. The major problem with this form of EDS revolves around the decision as to where the overall control of system interaction and processing is to reside.

The first possibility is to distribute processing and control such that both systems can operate independently and all interaction is via message passing. Because the two systems are effectively totally independent, however, inevitable problems arise in the areas of data integrity and redundancy.

A second possibility is to allow either the DBMS or the expert system to dominate. This is likely to be a more flexible architecture, but suffers from its inability to handle the addition of other subsystems satisfactorily.

Finally, we may envisage a system where processing is distributed, but control resides in an independent subsystem which manages the interaction between database and expert system. A simple example of this approach using a subsystem centred around a data dictionary has previously been discussed by the author (Beynon-Davies, 1987a, b). Perhaps a more sophisticated approach might vest control in something like a fifth-generation environment. This would extend the concept of an EDS to manage interactions between procedural programs, knowledge bases and databases. A number of commercially available products (KBMS, TOP-ONE) are already addressing these issues.

## Commercial possibilities

Expert database systems have an enormous scope for application within commercial DP. To give the reader a flavour for such developments, a select list of examples is given below for each of the types of EDS discussed.

### An enhanced database system

- Embedding. An example of an embedded deductive component might be a set of routines that validate complex data entry screens or maintain the logical integrity of a database. For example, the INGRES team are developing a front-end to their relational database which makes explicit use of the frame idea – a popular knowledge representation formalism (Beynon Davies, 1988c). Applications are envisaged as being built from a system of frames. Frames would be used to get data from the database and display it in a form. Conversely, they would be used to take data from a form and put it into the database. Frames will be allowed to call other frames, and do computations (Durham, 1988).
- Filtering. In a computer-assisted learning example, the deductive component might be used to run the interaction with the user and build up a model of user's performance from their use of the learning material in a database. This is one example of an intelligent front end to a

database. Another example is the number of natural language front-ends, such as INTELLECT, which presently exist within the commercial market.

- Interaction. A classic example of database–deductive component interaction is query optimisation. In a relational database system any query expressed in SQL – the emerging standard interface to RDBMS – can be performed in a number of different ways. The crucial criterion in choosing the best implementation of a query is the time it takes to respond to the user. It has been shown, for instance, that a relatively straightforward SQL query depending on the way it is implemented can take anything from 7 seconds to 2-3 days to respond to the user! (Date, 1986) Clearly, there is a need within any relational environment to build some intelligence into the system which decides upon the most appropriate implementation in any particular case.

Perhaps a more application-oriented example of DBMS – ES interaction is in the classic case of stock control. A prime area for the application of a set of deductive routines is in the reordering of stock. In conventional systems this is usually handled by placing a reorder level and reorder amount field in the stock record. When a reorder level is reached the reorder amount is ordered from a supplier.

Such fields represent the implicit codification of knowledge. Presumably, the stock control manager arrives at some appropriate figures for reorder level and reorder amount for each product in his system by considering a number of factors.

For instance:

- Size of product. Larger products take up more storage space. Consequently, lesser amounts of large products can be ordered and stored.
- Turnover of product. A large turnover of products should mean a high reorder level and amount.
- Value of product. The higher the value of, the product, presumably the lower the reorder level and amount are likely to be.
- Bulk buying. The more of a product that can be ordered at one time, the more likely a product is to benefit from bulk discount.

These and other factors might be incorporated into a knowledge base that feeds a value back to the ordering system. There are a number of benefits in this approach. For instance, such a value is likely to be more accurate than the deterministic value produced by the conventional approach. Also, the ordering knowledge in the system is now represented explicitly. It is therefore more amenable to inspection and modification.

## An enhanced expert system with external links

- Loosely coupled. Selection of customer records down loaded to a knowledge base for customer credit evaluation.
- Tightly coupled. An expert system for production scheduling which uses an external database of production management information. For example, there is a life insurance expert system that develops, recommends and explains customised life insurance policies. This expert system makes extensive use of an actuarial database (Jarke and Vessilion, 1984).

## Interdependent expert system and database

Within any large manufacturing organisation production management information probably exists in practice as an independent database perhaps used for production planning. An expert system for production scheduling can easily be added on to this database to handle areas that are normally the preserve of programs written from the angle of operations research (Maney and Reid, 1986).

## Conclusion

For knowledge engineering to take off as a commercial proposition, mainstream conventional data processing departments have to be exposed to the cutting edge of artificial intelligence. This can only be done to a limited extent by the application of stand-alone systems to the fringes of conventional computing. Intelligent software must be adopted to the task of cleaning up the exceptions that conventional systems cannot handle. This means embedding KBS within conventional systems, and allowing them to access databases and communicate their results to conventional procedural programs.

It is the author's belief that KBS will form an important part of the information systems of the future: not only in the sense of KBS embedded within conventional systems, but also in the whole notion of KBS applied to the problem of CASE. We shall discuss some of these issues in our concluding chapter.

# 15  Large-scale Methodologies

## Introduction

Previous chapters have been devoted to describing a number of techniques that fall under the auspices of contemporary systems analysis and design. Presenting the techniques as a set of relatively discrete entities has hopefully emphasised that the individual systems developer can usually select appropriate techniques as and when they are needed during the project life cycle. This means that because of the large number of choices available, a large number of possible development methodologies can be created (Hawryszkiewicz, 1988).

Although it is theoretically possible for a development methodology to be made up for each specific project, this is not normally the case in practice. Instead, a standard methodology is normally employed for all enterprise projects. This is done for a number of reasons:

1. Developers do not need to spend valuable time creating a new methodology for each new project. Instead, they become skilled in the application of techniques within one overarching framework.
2. New members of the development team are easily trained in the standard methodology.
3. A standard methodology facilitates communication not only between development staff, but also with end-users.

Any organisation looking to set up a standard methodology for systems development has a number of available choices:

1. It can develop its own.
2. It can purchase and use one of the many 'off-the-shelf' methodologies.
3. It can purchase an 'off-the-shelf' methodology but adapt it to its own purposes.

A development methodology, whether it be 'off-the-shelf' or bespoke, is made up of three primary components:

1. A set of techniques.
2. A documentation method associated with these techniques.

3. Some indication of how the techniques chosen along with the documentation method fit in to the typical project life cycle.

In previous chapters we have discussed some of the dominant techniques within the contemporary domain of systems analysis and design. This chapter is devoted first to discussing in general terms the three major types or paradigms of method-making presently available. We then move on to discuss the framework underlying one very popular contemporary methodology, namely SSADM, as an instance of what is available off-the-shelf.

## Data-structure and data-flow approaches

It is useful to classify the vast array of modern methodologies under two major headings (Fitzgerald et.al., 1985). First, those methodologies which are primarily concerned with database design. We shall collectively call these methodologies the data-structure approach. Second, those methodologies that emphasise the flow of information through some information system. We shall collectively call these the data-flow approach. As a general abstraction, it is probably true to say that the data-flow approach has had strong support from American software companies and their European associates, while the data-structure approach has perhaps had its strongest impact in Europe. We shall take a brief look at each of these approaches in turn.

## The data structure approach

A vast amount of literature has grown up around the topic of database design (Rock-Evans, 1981) (Bracket, 1987) (Vetter, 1987). Most of these approaches start by using the methods of data analysis, E–R diagrams and normalisation to arrive at an appropriate logical structure for a proposed database. This database is then validated against some notion of system requirements and 'flexed' to accommodate process concerns. At an informal level, this validation may simply involve listing a set of transactions that must be performed by the system, and checking these off one by one against a set of E–R diagrams or normalised table structures. At a more formal level it may involve drawing a complete set of ELHs to document how entities are actively involved in a system. The final stage in the exercise is to translate the logical and validated table structures that result (often referred to as a conceptual schema) into the physical structures and mechanisms used by a particular DBMS.

### The data-flow approach

The data-flow approach works in the opposite direction from the data-structure approach (Gane and Sarson, 1977, De-Marco, 1979a Yourdon and Constantine, 1979). It begins usually by drawing a set of DFDs that describe the current physical system. This set of diagrams is then 'logical-ised' in some way. That is, all references to the physical aspects of the existing system are removed. On the new logical set of DFDs a number of 'domains of change' are plotted. These constitute areas that reflect problems with the existing system or requirements for the new system. Using such domains, a new set of DFDs are drawn which attempt to model the workings of the new system at a logical level. The final stage involves translating this proposed logical system into a document which describes the physical implementation of the new system.

Although the primary technique used in this approach is the DFD, at least two other techniques are used to supplement the DFD hierarchy. At each phase in the development, for instance, a data dictionary is used to describe in more detail the data flows, data stores and processes making up the description of the information system. Descriptions of the data structures and elements making up logical data stores are then used to perform some data analysis, leading perhaps to concrete file specifications. In contrast, process descriptions in association with some medium such as structure charts are used to derive program specifications.

### Integrative methodologies

Data-structure methods can generally be said to suffer from an inadequate representation of information flow. Data-flow methodologies, on the other hand, do not satisfactorily address the problems of data structure. In response to these inadequacies, a number of recent methodologies have attempted to integrate these two different approaches to systems analysis and design. Perhaps the methodology which has received the greatest attention, at least in Britain, goes under the title SSADM (Structured Systems Analysis and Design Method).

### The need for SSADM

To reiterate some of the discussion in the introductory chapter, the development of large computer systems is undoubtedly one of the most complex, time-consuming and costly exercises undertaken by any organisation. Although, to quote one figure, the processing power of computer hardware per dollar spent has increased on average by 30 per cent per annum in the period since 1970, software productivity has increased only by an estimated 4-7 per cent per annum in the same period. This is clearly a large 'hardware-software' gap.

Over the last twenty years or so a number of proposals have been put forward as a solution to this software problem. In the late 1960s and early 1970s we had the structured programming movement. In the mid to late 1970s we had the fashion for structured design. More recently, that is, during the early 1980s, the vogue has been for structured analysis.

This chapter presents an overview of a methodology which has been influenced by all three of these movements. Although the paradigm uses the title Structured Systems Analysis and Design Methodology, SSADM for short, the objective is clearly to produce computer systems following many of the well-established tenets of structured programming.

## The history of SSADM

The history of SSADM is as follows. In 1980 a British consultancy, Learmonth and Burchett Management Systems (LBMS), were invited to work with the Central Computer and Telecommunications Agency (CCTA) in carrying out a joint project to develop a standard analysis and design method for central government. This resulted in SSADM which is now mandatory procedure for all UK government computing projects. LBMS market the method as LBMS Structured Development Method (LSDM) and have succeeded in interesting many commercial companies in aspects of the method (Cutts, 1987; Downs et al, 1987).

## The structure of SSADM

SSADM is organised into six clearly defined stages. These stages are subdivisions of two overarching phases from the software development life cycle, namely, systems analysis and design.

Systems analysis
– Analysis of current status and problems
– Specification of requirements
– Selection of a system option
Systems design
– Data design
– Process design
– Physical design

Each of these stages is defined in terms of:

1. The set of tasks to be performed in the stage.
2. The set of techniques to be used in the stage.
3. The inputs to the stage, and the outputs from the stage.

This is clearly what is meant by 'structure' as applied to systems analysis and design.

**Tasks**

Analysis

    Investigate the current system
    Create the current physical data-flow diagrams
    Create the current entity model
    Create the data-store/entity cross-reference
    Create the current logical data-flow diagrams
    Create the problems and requirements list
    User review

Specification

    Create the required logical data-flow diagrams
    Create the required entity model
    Document the entity descriptions
    Document the system input, system output and data-flow descriptions
    Document the function descriptions
    Create the entity function matrix
    Create the entity life histories
    User review

Selection of system options

    Postulate system options
    Review and select option
    Set the design constraints
    Review

Data design

    Select data structures
    Normalisation
    Create entity descriptions
    Create the entity model
    Compare and rationalise entity models
    Compare and rationalise entity descriptions

Process design
    Review the specification documentation
    Create the process catalogue
    Create the logical process outlines
    Review

Physical design
    Create the physical files/database specification
    Specify the access paths
    Create the program specifications
    Design tuning
    Create the implementation plan
    Create the user manual
    Create the operations manual

**Techniques**
Analysis
    Data-flow diagrams
    Entity models
    Cross-reference
    Walkthroughs and documentation

Specification
    Data-flow diagrams
    Entity models
    Cross-reference
    Entity life histories
    Walkthroughs and documentation

Selection of system options
    Data-flow diagrams
    Walkthroughs and documentation

Data design
    Normalisation
    Entity models
    Walkthroughs and documentation

Process design
    Process outlines
    Walkthroughs and documentation

Physical design
   Physical design control
   Walkthroughs and documentation

**Inputs and outputs**
Analysis
   Input
      Terms of reference
      Feasibility study report (optional)
   Output
      Current logical data-flow diagrams
      Current entity model
      Problems and requirements list

Specification of requirements
   Input
      Current logical data-flow diagrams
      Current entity model
      Problems and requirements list
   Output
      Required logical data-flow diagrams
      Required entity model
      Entity descriptions
      Input and output descriptions
      Function descriptions
      Entity function matrix
      Entity life histories

Selection of system option
   Input
      Required logical data-flow diagrams
   Output
      Required physical data-flow diagrams

Logical data design
   Input
      Required physical data-flow diagrams
      Required entity model
      Entity descriptions
      Input and output descriptions
   Output
      Logical entity model
      Logical entity descriptions

Logical process design
  Input
    Required physical data-flow diagrams
    Logical entity model
    Logical entity descriptions
    Function descriptions
    Entity function matrix
    Entity life histories
  Output
    Logical process outlines

Physical design
  Input
    Logical process outlines
    Logical entity model
    Logical entity descriptions
  Output
    Program specifications
    Database or file specifications
    An implementation plan
    A user manual
    An operations manual

## SSADM and project control

It must be said that SSADM is not a project-control system; it does, however, provide a structure by which projects may be planned and monitored.

Since each stage and task within SSADM is given a specific objective or range of objectives, and each stage and task is defined by a given set of deliverables, the monitoring process is made much easier. A stage or task is complete when the documented output has been produced and agreed. Similarly, each stage or task may commence only when the required inputs are available.

## Conclusion

SSADM is generally recognised to be one of the best sets of traditional standards for systems analysis and design in data processing. The methodology divides systems development into stages which all produce standard documents to summarise progress and serve as the basis for the next stage.

The stages correspond roughly to the ideal of defining the application in business terms, defining it in computer terms, building a system, and installing a system.

There are few loose ends in the methodology. No documents are included which are not needed, and there is always a document with an unambiguous meaning where there is likely to be some misunderstanding between members of the project team.

The main question about SSADM, however, arises from the fact that it does not incorporate elements which could handle developments in the computing world since its conception in 1980. We are here of course referring to the fact that fourth-generation technology (4GLs, RDBMSs, etc, has made possible the rapid development of systems (see chapter 15).

SSADM is clearly designed as a tool for the analysis of 'well-structured' environments. This usually means environments where there is at least some form of existing manual system which needs computerisation. In areas not so well structured, the advantages of rapid prototyping become of utmost importance.

The basic message of SSADM remains valid. If it is to remain a standard into the early 1990s, however, it needs updating to take account of the elements of fourth-generation technology.

# 16 Rapid Prototyping

## Introduction

In the introductory chapter we discussed the standard life-cycle or 'water-fall' model of software development. This model is generally held to be an excellent vehicle for the generation of information systems from well-defined environments. A well-defined environment is usually one where there is some form of existing manual system waiting to be computerised.

The life-cycle model has, however, proved inadequate for handling ill-defined environments. An ill-defined environment is one where there are probably no existing manual procedures. There is merely a general demand for some solution to a problem, which may be ill-structured. For such environments, a more informal approach to systems development has been suggested. This informal approach, which we shall generally call *proto-typing*, is the subject of the present chapter.

Prototyping is essentially the process of building a model of the proposed system. Normally using a fourth-generation language or environment, the systems analyst, after some initial investigation, constructs a working model which is demonstrated to the user. The analyst and the user discuss the prototype, agreeing on enhancements and amendments. The ease of use of most 4GLs means that the analyst can quickly make the suggested improvements in the working model. This cycle of inspection–discussion–amendment is repeated several times until the user is satisfied with the model. When this stage is reached, the building of the true system can commence (Dearnley and Mayhew,1983).

## Types of prototyping

It is useful to identify at least three different kinds of prototype:

- *Mock-up*: a single-screen or multi-screen model of how a significant part of the proposed system (usually the user interface) will work.
- *Research model*: an investigation of crucial parts of the system which will prove an important factor in performance issues etc.
- *Implementation model*: an investigation into the different possible

169

ways that a system may be physically implemented; that is, in terms of languages, DBMSs or hardware.

## Benefits of prototyping

Prototyping has two major benefits in software development:

- *Clarifying requirements.* In software development the user is often heard to say something like: 'I don't know what I want until I see it'. Prototyping allows the user to refine his ideas on what the system should look like. The nature of prototyping is that it allows users to be wrong. The fact that users can change their minds is a recognised and indeed encouraged part of the process (Giddings, 1984). As a result of this, the analyst gets a better understanding of what the user wants. The primary objective of prototyping then is to clarify requirements. Prototyping eliminates suprises at the end of the development cycle, as users have seen and agreed what will be delivered.
- *Improving productivity.* All these benefits lead to the fact that prototyping has enormous potential for improving productivity. This it can do in two ways. First, the improved quality of the requirements document can have direct returns in shortening the back-end of the project life cycle – particularly the testing stages. Second, substantial parts of the prototype may be suitable as a base for the final system, thus cutting down the effort involved in programming and testing.

## Problems with prototyping

The major problem with prototyping lies in identifying precisely what it is. Is prototyping concerned solely with system specification, or can it be used as the basis for system production?

In many other professions, for example, mechanical engineering, it is taken for granted that the prototype will eventually be thrown away. In DP, there is much discussion as to whether the developed prototype should itself become part of, or even the whole of, the finalised system.

- *The 'prefab' problem.* If the 4GL being used is sufficiently powerful and flexible to make 3GL coding unnecessary, there may be a strong case for effectively implementing a prototype as it stands. What often happens however, is that prototyping initiates the 'prefab' problem. Because the user wants the system quickly, the prototype is implemented on a temporary basis. Many important things are left undone; for example proper recovery and restart procedures, proper test planning, proper sizing etc. As with emergency prefabricated housing, the intention is to replace the prototype with something more substantial quite soon. However, because of other pressing problems, the implemented prototype, with all its inadequacies remains in production.

- *The documentation problem.* The nature of prototyping, where documentation follows on from the system, rather than coming before it, means that there is also the risk of a prototype continuing into production undocumented. Associated with this is the problem that large-scale prototypes can become unmanageable through repeated iterations. The lack of documentation and repeated change can so affect the system that the time taken to make further changes increases unacceptably.
- *The problem of cumulative change.* Over a period of years, the cumulative effect of changes to a traditional system can make it harder and harder to implement further changes as the initial sound structure of the system becomes more and more compromised. A prototype taken through to implementation may show similar characteristics, as it has been subject to repeated change during development. The difference is that the system derived from a prototype is already several years 'old' when implemented.
- *The problem of planning.* Perhaps the greatest problem however is that, due to the open-ended nature of the exercise, there is a great difficulty in providing accurate estimating and resource planning for prototyping. This is a serious problem given that most commercial software projects have to justify themselves financially.

## Effective prototyping

To prototype effectively one must therefore consider four major issues: who, how, where, and when.

### Who should prototype?

A prototyping effort is best used by analysts who are well informed about the prototyping approach. The increased interaction between analyst and user characteristic of prototyping demands people skilled in human communication (Alavi, 1984).

### How to prototype?

Prototyping should never be used instead of good project management. Prototyping may well alter the project life cycle, especially because of the way in which it facilitates iterative improvement. What it does not do is replace the project life cycle. There is still the need for strong project management and the application of a structured systems analysis and design methodology.

### Where to prototype?

If prototyping is to be incorporated into structured systems analysis and design, it should clearly be identified primarily as a means for systems specification. The additional knowledge about user requirements generated by the prototyping exercise is clearly invaluable. At some point in the development process, however, prototyping must be terminated. This is probably best done before the user requirements document is produced. Constraining prototyping in this manner at the design stage means that more informed decisions can be made about the appropriateness of using various parts of the prototyping exercise in the final design of a system.

### When to prototype?

Prototyping is best used in the face of unclear or ambiguous user requirements. Prototyping seems to be effective in dealing with undecided users and in clarifying 'fuzzy' requirements.

# 17 Information Engineering

## Introduction

In recent years it has become clear that information is a resource of high value to organisations. In this sense, data are viewed as a corporate asset and therefore must be managed in the same way as any other organisational resource.

In other words, information resource management or stategic data planning pertains to data in the same way as human resource management pertains to people (Martin, 1982). Data, like people, are subject to sound management principles. They are subject to organisation, planning, control, inventory, cost-accounting and budgeting.

In this chapter we consider the two keystones of information engineering: the building of a corporate information architecture and the founding of organisational data processing in the information centre concept.

## Building a corporate information architecture

Information resource management is emerging as a formal discipline for managing the data needed to support the activities of a business. Its aim is to develop a complete corporate information architecture. This architecture establishes the definition and structure of a company's data. It defines a logical and physical data model for the entire enterprise.

A number of stages have been identified as important in building this architecture.

1. Gaining management commitment. That is, getting management committed to, and involved in, the management of the information resource. Managers are required to set both the long-term and short-term information needs of the organisation. They must set priorities based on these needs and establish plans for achieving goals. They must also allocate budgets to carry out such plans.
2. Development of a global information plan. This is done top-down in much the same way as one would develop any information system. Two global logical models are developed: a model for the activities of

the enterprise (enterprise activity model), and a model for the data needed to support organisational activities (enterprise data model). From these logical models a physical model is attempted by grouping data into subject databases and systems.

3. Development of detailed information plans. For each subject database and system a detailed plan is constructed for its development, implementation and maintenance.

4. Setting up a data administration function.

5. Creating the information centre.

### Developing an enterprise activity model

An enterprise activity model is a high-level description of the activities of an organisation. It is built up in a number of steps:

1. List the functional areas of the business. These are the major areas of activity in the organisation. For example,

   FINANCE
   PERSONNEL
   SALES
   DISTRIBUTION
   etc.

2. Each functional area carries out a certain number of processes. The next step is to identify the processes involved in each function. For instance,

   FINANCE
      financial planning
      capital acquisition
      funds management

   SALES
      territory management
      selling
      sales administration
      customer relations

   PERSONNEL
      personnel planning
      recruiting
      compensation planning

A large complex organisation might have as many as 30 functions and 150 to 300 processes.

3. Identify, for each process, the typical activities that are needed to run each process. There are typically 5 to 30 activities for each business process. For example, for a purchasing process we might have the following list of activities:

Create requisitions for purchase.
Select suppliers.
Create purchase orders.
Follow up the delivery of items on purchase orders.
Process exceptions.
Prepare information for accounts payable.
Record supplier performance data.
Analyse supplier performance.

All this should sound somewhat familiar. Enterprise activity modelling is really an attempt to apply the partitioning process characteristic of techniques such as data-flow diagramming to the global aspects of an organisation's information. This is in contrast to a subset of an organisation's activity to which they are normally applied. DFD's can therefore form a useful part of the documentation of the corporate information architecture.

### Developing an enterprise data model

Alongside a dynamic picture of the organisation we need a static picture of the data needed to support the activities of the organisation. This enterprise data model is built up in the following way:

1. For each functional area of the business, identify the entities of interest to that function. For instance, purchasing might be interested in the following entities:

PART
SUPPLIER
REQUISITION

2. From the entire list of entities cluster the entities into subject databases. Subject databases relate to classes of data of interest to the organisation rather than to conventional computer applications.

A technique such as E–R diagramming and logical data dictionaries are of obvious relevance to this process. In a sense, what we are attempting to do in constructing an enterprise data model is to draft an E–R diagram or logical data dictionary for the entire organisation. From such a global information map we then derive an appropriate database structure into which we feed the attributes of interest to the organisation.

## Group subject databases into systems

This involves plotting subject databases in our enterprise data model against the processes from the enterprise activity model. This is fundamentally a larger-scale version of the entity function matrix described in chapter 8. For example, consider the matrix illustrated.

| SUBJECT DATABASES PROCESSES | Customers | Suppliers | Sales | Employees | Products |
|---|---|---|---|---|---|
| Accounting | X | X | | X | |
| Purchasing | | X | | | X |
| Territory management | X | | X | | |
| Selling | X | | X | | X |
| Customer relations | X | | X | | |
| Personnel planning | | | | X | |

From this matrix, we then identify clusters of entities and processes which could usefully form the basis for information systems. This means rearranging the order of either processes and/or subject databases on our axes until some form of aggregation occurs.

## Data administration

Once a corporate information architecture has been implemented in some form, there still remains the problem of administering the data on a day-to-day basis. The effective management of the data resource begins with the establishment of a formal data administration function.

Administration of data must begin with a resource inventory: a large physical data dictionary. In its simplest form, this provides a list of the data that exist in the company, who owns the data, and where they are located. This list must be supplemented by a set of logical data and activity models which indicate at a high level the corporate information policy. All of this constitutes meta data. Data administration manages the meta data of the company: the data about data.

Administration of data also includes data security and integrity. The data must be kept secure from unauthorised access, alteration and destruction. The data must also, however, be secure against authorised access, in the sense that control must be exercised over what part of the corporate database is to be maintained by what corporate function.

Finally, data administration must be involved in the access function. It must ensure that data are available when and where the user needs those data. This will often involve the administrator in being concerned with the transmission of data along data communication lines, and the security and integrity of such data during transmission.

## The information centre

In response to the integrative emphasis of the information engineering approach, many modern DP departments have cast themselves either entirely or in part as 'information centres'. An information centre is a corpus of DP expertise whose role is to service other departments which are heavily involved in handling a large proportion of their DP themselves. This is in marked contrast to the traditional role of the DP department as the mono-polistic controller of all organisational data processing.

## Objectives

The major objective of the information centre is to speed up the develop-ment of applications required by end-users. This is achieved by providing a fast turnaround for user requests and fulfilling the *ad hoc* information needs of the organisation.

Providing a quick response to user requests improves user satisfaction. It also reduces maintenance programming by shifting the mechanism for the production of 'run-of-of-the-mill' applications such as one-shot analyses, special reports, etc., out of third-generation technology into the fourth-generation arena.

## Mechanisms

The information centre (IC) is normally implemented by setting up a specialised group of software professionals devoted to the use of fourth-generation technology such as query languages, report generators, spread-sheets, etc. Users are also usually given in-depth training in the use of these fourth-generation products. The IC concept is also founded around the notion of distributed computing, that is, siting computing resources where they are needed. This primarily means connecting up personal computers, mini computers and mainframes in an effective organisational network.

### Changes

All this means that there is a change in the role of DP staff. The traditional distinction between systems analysts and programmers becomes eroded. There is a corresponding broadening of the technical expertise needed by computing staff. The change is from the systems analyst's technical role to a business analyst's company role.

The information centre concept also stimulates a change in the relationship between end-users and the DP department. End-users become much more involved in their own DP and are expected to solve most of their run-of-the-mill problems themselves. The DP department casts itself more as a consultancy centre for information technology-advising, training and helping users to perform their own DP work.

### Control

Having an information centre does not mean that one can forego management control and planning of a corporate information policy. In fact, probably more such planning and control is needed. There is still a strong need, for instance, for a data administration function. The corporate database has to be organised effectively to handle the heavy demands made of it under the aegis of the information centre concept.

### Conclusion

In this chapter we have discussed the way in which information resource management (IRM) or strategic data planning is really an activity subject to the same exigencies that characterise normal information systems development (see figure 17.1). The primary difference is one of scale. Information engineering is clearly a methodology devoted to the global business concerns of an organisation. It seeks to identify an appropriate corporate information architecture – a framework within which everyday systems development takes its place.

Most of the systems analysis techniques that we have discussed are equally applicable to information engineering as they are to normal information systems development. Data-flow diagrams, for instance, can clearly be 'levelled' to cope with the larger complexity of IRM problems. A recent paper by Feldman and Miller (1986) has demonstrated how E–R diagrams can similarly be partitioned to cope with corporate information system architectures.

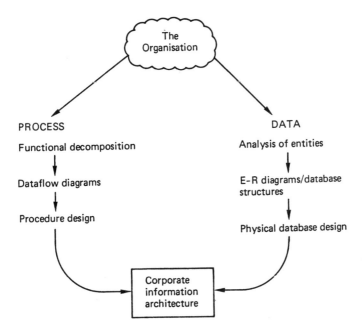

*Figure 17.1*

# 18   The Future of Information Systems Development

## Introduction

Prediction or prophesy is an ill-defined art rather than a systematic science. Any attempt to predict the future by extrapolating from present trends is unlikely to be even remotely accurate. Nevertheless, it is important to close this book with some indication of the short- and long-term future of information systems development, even if this may largely reflect the hopes and aspirations of the author.

In the opening sections of this book we discussed the importance of logical modelling for contemporary systems analysis and design. We then moved on to discuss a range of techniques (E–R diagramming, DFDs etc.) whose overall aim is to facilitate the modelling of information systems. The section on tools devoted its attention to the growing CASE movement which takes as its central theme the provision of higher-level software for systems development. Finally, in the section on the organisation of systems development we discussed contemporary methodologies and the important effect that the 'structuredness' of the studied environment has on the selection of a particular methodology.

We begin the conclusion of this book therefore with an overall premise which expresses the dominant theme running through each of these facets of modern computing. That information systems development is primarily a task of conceptual modelling: a process of successive refinement through three levels of information model. That systems analysis is logical modelling, that systems design is physical modelling and that system implementation is computational modelling.

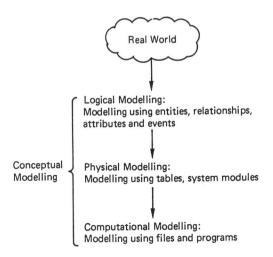

A database, for instance, is a model of an evolving real world. The state of this model, at a given instant, represents the knowledge that it has acquired from this world. But as Sowa cogently puts it:

> ...models are abstractions of reality. The systems analyst or database administrator must play the role of philosopher–king in determining what knowledge to represent, how to organise and express it and what constraints to impose to keep it a consistent, faithful model of the outside world. To do a good job in analysing reality, a systems analyst must be sensitive to semantic issues and have a working knowledge of conceptual structures (Sowa, 1984).

Given that information systems development is fundamentally a task of conceptual modelling, the primary area of research directed at such development attempts to bring the three levels of conceptual modelling closer together. The eventual aim of many CASE tools is to enable the systems analyst to produce logical models (systems analyses) that bear some relationship to physical models, and physical models (system designs) that can then be automatically translated into computational models (information systems). The rest of this chapter is devoted to examining some of this fundamental research in more detail.

## Conceptual modelling

The growing demand for systems of ever-increasing complexity has stimulated the demand for higher-level concepts, tools and techniques in every area of computing. Some of these areas, in particular artificial intelligence, databases and programming languages are attempting to meet this demand by defining a new, more abstract, level of system description often referred to as the conceptual level (Brodie *et al.*, 1984).

In Artificial Intelligence, the problem of building an 'intelligent' system is seen primarily as the problem of representing knowledge about some domain of interest. Knowledge representation is therefore a central theme of AI research. In the last few years database researchers have concentrated on developing semantic data models. A semantic data model is a database design which more naturally models the workings of some organisation. In programming languages abstraction has been the key issue. Abstraction is the process of specifying implementation-independent packages of data, functions and control.

To emphasise the common goals of these three research efforts, a new integrative activity called conceptual modelling has been proposed. This chapter attempts briefly to discuss the developments within AI, databases and programming languages that will form the bedrock of this endeavour.

## Knowledge representation

Artificial Intelligence gained a name and an area of focus at the US Dartmouth Conference in the summer of 1956 (Mccorduck, 78). The first period of AI research stimulated by this conference, was dominated by the belief that a few general problem-solving strategies implemented on a computer could produce expert-level performance in a particular domain. As such research developed it was soon realised that such general-purpose mechanisms were too weak to solve most complex problems.

In reaction to these limitations, researchers began to concentrate on more narrowly defined problems. By the mid 1970s, a number of expert systems had begun to emerge: DENDRAL, MYCIN, PROSPECTOR, INTERNIST to name but a few. In 1977, Ed Feigenbaum presented the key insight into the power of the expert systems approach (Feigenbaum, 1977). He maintained that the power of an expert system derives not from the particular formalisms and inference mechanisms that it uses, but from the knowledge it possesses. Knowledge, and not problem solving strategy, is the important thing. It is for this reason that an expert system is often referred to as one, very successful, example of a knowledge based system (KBS).

One of the fundamental problems of AI therefore is the development of a sufficiently precise and fruitful notation with which to represent knowledge. A number of knowledge representation schemes have been proposed: logic, production rules, frames, semantic nets. As yet no single scheme has achieved an overwhelming dominance, but particularly because of its association with database work, first-order logic looks promising.


## Logic and databases

Ever since Codd brought out his seminal (1970) paper on the relational data model researchers have been fascinated with the application of formal logic to databases. This is probably because formal logic has a number of advantages for use in database work (Kowalski, 1979):

1. It acts as a rigorous formalism for assessing the informalisms of conventional database work. As such, it has proved to be a useful vehicle for making explicit some of the hidden assumptions underlying conventional database practice.
2. The same formalism can be used for representing various elements that in conventional database systems require a number of different formalisms. For example:

   - defining data.
   - expressing queries on data.
   - expressing integrity constraints.
   - extending conventional databases with deductive facilities.

This section acts as a brief introduction to the application of logic in database systems. It is intended to give the reader a flavour of some of the advantages mentioned above.


## A relational database

Suppose we are interested in representing information from the classic suppliers/parts/shipments example (Date, 1986). As a relational database this information would be represented as three tables as follows.

```
SUPPLIERS (sno, sname, status, city)
           ---

PARTS (pno, pname, colour, weight, city)
       ---

SHIPMENTS (sno, pno, qty)
           ---  ---
```

```
SUPPLIERS                              SHIPMENTS

SNO   SNAME   STATUS   CITY       SNO   PNO   QTY
---   -----   ------   ----       ---   ---   ---
s1    smith   20       london     s1    p1    300
s2    jones   10       paris      s1    p2    200
s4    blake   30       paris      s1    p3    400
s3    clarke  20       london     s1    p4    200
s5    adams   30       athens     s1    p5    100
                                  s1    p6    100
                                  s2    p1    200
                                  s2    p2    400
                                  s3    p2    200
                                  s4    p2    200
                                  s4    p4    300
                                  s4    p5    400


PARTS

PNO   PNAME   COLOUR   WEIGHT   CITY
---   -----   ------   ------   ----
p1    nut     red      12       london
p2    bolt    green    17       paris
p3    screw   blue     17       rome
p4    screw   red      14       london
p5    cam     blue     12       paris
p6    cog     red      19       london
```

## A logic database

Alternatively, we can represent the above information as a logic database:

```
S(s1, smith, 20, london).      SP(s1, p1, 300).
S(s2, jones, 10, paris).       SP(s1, p2, 200).
S(s4, blake, 30, paris).       SP(s1, p3, 400).
S(s3, clarke, 20, london).     SP(s1, p4, 200).
S(s5, adams, 30, athens).      SP(s1, p5, 100).
                               SP(s1, p6, 100).
                               SP(s2, p1, 200).
                               SP(s2, p2, 400).
                               SP(s3, p2, 200).
                               SP(s4, p2, 200).
                               SP(s4, p4, 300).
                               SP(s4, p5, 400).
```

```
P(p1, nut, red, 12, london).
P(p2, bolt, green, 17, paris).
P(p3, screw, blue, 17, rome).
P(p4, screw, red, 14, london).
P(p5, cam, blue, 12, paris).
P(p6, cog, red, 19, london).
```

These are the facts or assertions expressed about the Suppliers database. Each fact is made up of a 'predicate' – S, SP, or P – and a number of constants – p1, s4, 200 etc.

## Views

We can also express a number of rules on this database in a form of logic known as Horn clause form as follows:

```
LONDON_S(X,Y,Z) :- S(X,Y,Z,london).
MAJOR_S(X) :- SP(X,p2,Y),
Y >= 300.
```

Rules are made up of a mixture of predicates, constants, variables (X, Y etc.) and logical connectives. ':-' represents the 'implies' connective. The MAJOR_S rules states that 'if a supplier X supplies part p2 and ships over 300 of p2 then this implies that X is a major supplier'.

These rules are what are conventionally known as 'views' on the suppliers database. In other words, they express how to form virtual tables from the base information in the database. The first view produces information on all London suppliers. The second view generates a subset of major suppliers for part p2 with shipments over 300. This means that the rules above implicitly define two new relations:

```
LONDON_S(sno,sname,status)
MAJOR_S(sno)
```

Rules such as these turn a conventional database into a deductive database (Lloyd, 1983). A conventional relational database consists of a collection of facts. A deductive database contains not only facts but also rules. This enables it to make deductions, that is, generate new facts from facts already existing in the database. We can deduce for instance which suppliers are major suppliers by application of the MAJOR_S rule above.

### Queries

One implicit assumption underlying conventional relational database work which has been made explicit through the application of logic is the distinction between a closed and an open query expressed on a database. A closed query simply requires a YES/NO or TRUE/FALSE response. For instance, a closed query expressed on the supplier's database might be:

```
'Did supplier S1 ship 300 of part P1?'
```

This can be expressed in logic as:

```
:- SP(s1,p1,300).
```

and would evaluate to yes or true in terms of a match with our database.

An open query requires a set of records as a response. Suppose for instance we wish to express the following query on our database:

```
'list all the suppliers for part p2'
```

A conventional SQL version of this would be:

```
SELECT sname
FROM s,sp
WHERE s.sno = sp.sno
  AND sp.pno = 'p2'
```

We express this in logic as:

```
:-ANSWER(Y)
ANSWER(Y):-SP(X,p2,U),
           S(X,Y,Z,W).
```

Suppose, however, that a variant of this query finds that there are no suppliers for a given part. What does this mean? The conventional interpretation relies on another implicit assumption made explicit by logic work. This assumption, known variously as the 'closed world assumption' or 'negation as failure', states that in a non-deductive database any relationship between objects which is not represented explicitly is assumed not to hold. A database is a computational model of the 'real world' in which only explicit facts are held to be true.

## Integrity constraints

Since data often contain errors, integrity constraints are used to describe properties which the data need to satisfy for the data to be correct.

Suppose we want to ensure that all London suppliers ship part p2 in sufficient quantities. In other words we want to ensure that all London suppliers are major suppliers. We can represent this as a rule in our database as follows:

```
MAJOR_S(X):-LONDON_S(X,Y,Z).
```

That is, 'if x is a London supplier then x is a major supplier'.

## Second order knowledge based system

Note that the integrity constraint above uses two rules which we previously defined as being views on our database. In a logic database the distinction between different types of rules becomes largely irrelevant. A view can be regarded as an integrity constraint and an integrity constraint can be regarded as a special type of view. This is the primary point of the exercise: that logic acts as a uniform formalism for representing a vast array of database concerns, both in terms of conventional databases and databases with deductive facilities. This makes logic a uniform or orthogonal formalism for knowledge representation. In terms of our distinction made in chapter 14 logic is a means for building second order knowledge based systems (Lloyd, 1983).

## Semantic data models

Data models are central to information systems. Data models provide the conceptual basis for thinking about data-intensive applications (Tsitchizris, 1982). They also provide a formal basis for tools and techniques used in developing information systems.

As discussed in chapter 3, any data model is made up of three components:

1. A collection of data structures for representing objects, attributes and the relationships between objects;
2. A collection of operators for transforming objects;
3. A set of general integrity rules which define valid database states and valid transitions between database states.

Using this approach there can usefully be said to be three generations of data models:

1. Primitive data models. Objects are represented as records grouped in files. Operations provided are primitive read and write operations over records.
2. Classic data models. The classic data models are the hierachical, network and relational data models. The hierarchical model is a direct extension of the file model above, while the network model is a superset of the hierarchical approach. The relational model is a significant departure from the hierarchical and network models and has proved influential in recent years (chapters 2 and 3).
3. Semantic data models. These models attempt to use richer and more expressive concepts to capture more meaning than is possible using the classic data models (Peckham and Maryanski, 1988).

It is the purpose of this section to give the reader some understanding of what is meant by the term semantic data model (SDM) and what advantages semantic data models have over the more traditional relational data model.

**The problem of semantics**

The relational data model has undoubtedly provided database practitioners with a modelling methodology independent of physical implementation concerns. Many people believe however that the relational model does not offer a sufficiently rich set of constructs for modelling the 'real world'. The past decade has therefore seen the emergence of a large range of alternative models. This collection of data models can be loosely categorised as 'semantic' since their one unifying characteristic is that they attempt to provide more meaningful content than the relational model.

**An example semantic data model**

Semantic data models are conceptual data models. That is, they are primarily models expressed in abstract or theoretical terms, much in the sense that the original relational data model was expressed. Just like the relational data model, however, a number of semantic data models have achieved a practical realisation. We therefore discuss here as an example of a practical implementation of an SDM the GENERIS system developed by a number of researchers at the University of Strathclyde and now marketed by Deductive Systems Ltd (Russell, 86).

GENERIS is a practical realisation of the entity-relationship approach to information modelling as advocated by Chen (1976). In this data model, the 'real world' is modelled in terms of entities, relationships and attributes.

Entities represent objects in the 'real world'. For instance, an employee and department may be entities important to some organisation. Relationships represent named associations between entities. A department employs many employees. Attributes represent the properties that characterise particular entities. Employee number and employee name might characterise an employee; department number and department name might characterise a department (see chapter 5).

One important type of relationship in the GENERIS system is the class membership relationship (referred to as a generic association). Using this relationship one entity can be made a member of another. That is, one entity becomes a class containing the other.

Let us assume for instance that an employee of an organisation is characterised by three defining attributes: name, age and the department that the employee works for. In the relational model, the employee entity would be represented by a table, and each of these attributes becomes a column name. In GENERIS however each attribute acts as a class for all data items in the attribute column. This has a number of advantages over the relational model.

The relationships between classes and entities fulfil the function of an index in a conventional system. A record can be located directly through any value in any class. This has the effect of maintaining a dynamic index on each column in a table. An employee record can be located by employee name, age and/or department.

Unlike a conventional index, however, a generic association is totally transparent to the user. Indexes do not have to be explicitly built and maintained. They are implicitly built and maintained by the GENERIS system itself when a table is created and used.

This also enables a significant simplification of queries run on a GENERIS database. Suppose we wished to find the age and department of an employee called John Smith. A conventional SQL query for this would look something like:

```
SELECT employee, department, age
FROM employees
WHERE employee = 'John Smith'
```

A GENERIS version of the same query would be:

```
DISPLAY department and age for John Smith
```

In other words, first, the GENERIS system does not have to be told that the relevant data is stored in the employees table. It knows that the attributes referred to in the query are stored there. Second, it does not have to be told that John Smith is an employee. The generic associations in the data tell it that.

This is fundamentally what we mean when we say that GENERIS is an implementation of a semantic data model. It is a database representation which incorporates more knowledge about meaningful relationships between data.

## Advantages of semantic data models

As the number of semantic data models has grown, so a number of benefits associated with these types of model has become clear:

1. Economy of expression. SDMs can represent exactly the same information as the relational model. Much of the information can be extracted however with greater ease.
2. Integrity maintenance. In the relational model most integrity constraints must be enforced explicitly through a set of data validation routines expressed on the database. SDMs provide a greater range of facilities for the implicit maintenance of database integrity.
3. Modelling flexibility. Most traditional data models provide only one mechanism for representing data. SDMs, primarily through their use of abstraction, allow the user to model and view data on many different levels.
4. Modelling efficiency. Because of their high-level nature, SDMs allow the user a more natural progression from conceptual model to computational model.

## The likely importance of SDMs

The first research papers on semantic data modelling only started to appear some seven years after Codd's seminal description of the relational model. It could be argued that it is only quite recently that the relational model has achieved a pre-eminence in database terms. It is therefore unlikely that systems based on semantic data modelling ideas will overtake the relational model in the short term. Nevertheless, if only because SDMs represent one branch of the convergence of the conceptual modelling work in AI, databases and programming languages, they are likely to have an enormous impact on the information systems of the future.

**Abstraction in modern programming languages**

A dominant theme in the development of modern programming languages is the development of tools for dealing with abstraction. An abstraction is a simplified description of a system that emphasises some of the systems details while suppressing others. During recent years most research activity in abstraction as applied to programming languages has been identified with the concept of an abstract data type. An abstract data type is a module consisting of a data structure and the operations associated with this data structure. The objective is to treat these modules in much the same way as the programmer treats ordinary data types such as integers or reals. An abstract data type therefore effectively extends the set of types available to a program (Shaw, 1984).

A particularly rich kind of abstract data type definition allows one abstraction to take another abstraction as a parameter. These generic definitions provide a large amount of modelling flexibility for the programmer. For instance, consider the problem of defining data types for an application that uses three kinds of unordered sets: sets of integers, sets of reals, and sets of user-defined points in three-dimensional space. Abstraction involves separating out the properties of unordered sets from the properties of their elements and representing them as follows:

```
TYPE unorderedset(T: type) is ...

VAR
        counters: unorderedset(integer)
        sizes: unorderedset(real)
        places: unorderedset(pointin3space)
```

A number of contemporary programming languages provide some or all of the facilities needed to support abstract data types. These include Pascal, Modula-2 and Ada.


**Declarative programming**

Perhaps the most profound impact on future information systems engineering will come from applying abstractive principles not solely to data and data types, but to the whole realm of programming. The premise of this section is that the future of computing is likely to be characterised by an increasing emphasis on a more declarative approach to systems development.

Declarative programming languages are a family of languages that are fundamentally different from the conventional imperative or procedural languages commonly in use in industry. When we program in an imperative or procedural language such as Pascal, COBOL or BASIC, we are machine oriented. That is, we prescribe the manner in which we want the processor to go about solving the problem. We explicitly specify the detailed flow of control necessary to carry out a given computation. In declarative languages we simply describe the logical structure of the problem to be solved. We leave the question of control largely up to the interpreter for the language.

Let us examine this contrast in more detail.

Programming might be described as the activity of representing some algorithm in some computer language. Kowalski maintains that any algorithm can be regarded as being made up of two components: a logic component and a control component (Kowalski, 1979). The logic component specifies the knowledge to be used in solving the problem. The control component represents the problem-solving strategies by means of which the knowledge is used.

In an imperative or procedural program, the logic and control components are necessarily intertwined. An ideal declarative program, in contrast, represents solely the logic component. This leaves open the possibility of finding the most efficient representation of the control component for the given declarative representation.

Declarative languages have been highly regarded in academic circles for a number of years. However, because they are often regarded as inefficient computationally, they have yet to achieve widespread commercial acceptance. Having said this, there are a number of reasons why declarative languages or the declarative approach will probably have a significant impact on the future development of commercial computing.

### Hardware developments

Most currently available computers are equivalent architecturally to the first machines built back in the 1940s. One central processor is connected to a large memory by a bus that is one byte wide. This is conventionally known as the Von Neumann architecture. Every breakthrough in hardware is used primarily to increase the capabilities of this architecture. The original rationale behind the architecture, namely the high ratio of processor cost to memory cost, has been eroded by hardware developments. Many people have therefore suggested that we build computers that reflect more clearly the fact that because modern processors and memory are built from roughly the same technology, they are roughly comparable in price. This makes it possible to build computers as networks of general-purpose processors, each of which can take a share of the large processing load which is the norm in modern systems.

To handle these new machines however we need appropriate software to manage the parallel execution of processes, sometimes known as concurrency. New languages such as Modula-2 and Ada have constructs which allow the programmer to initiate and control mutiple concurrent tasks. As the number of tasks that need to be handled concurrently multiplies, though, parallel processing becomes less practical to program conventionally.

Just as the procedural languages that we use reflect the conventional architecture, so a new type of language is needed to describe problems in a way that can be solved concurrently. Many people hold great hope for declarative languages in this direction.

## Software developments

Much research has gone into investigating program productivity. Two findings from such research have done much to change the face of software development.

The first is that no matter what programming language is used, any given programmer produces roughly the same number of lines of code; an average of 1500 lines of code per year. The implication of this finding is that the more powerful or high-level the language used, the more productive the programmer becomes. In other words, the more computing power that can be packaged within the constructs of a language, the easier it is to produce systems with such languages. Thus, over the years we have seen the trend towards higher-level programming languages (4GLs, etc.).

The second area of research has identified elements within programs that are particularly prone to error. This has led to the development of new languages that consciously eliminate such elements – the so-called structured languages. For instance, structured languages prohibit the use of elements such as the GOTO statement and global data, both of which have been shown to cause unwanted problems in software development. Such languages also encourage programmers to build systems out of well-defined and hence manageable modules which communicate with each other only through the passing of parameters (see chapter 10).

## Referential transparency

One of the major emphases of the structured approach is the attempt to improve the correspondence between the specification of a problem and the implementation of a solution in terms of a computer program. Making a specification more precise in this manner usually means searching for ways to make unambiguous statements about what a program should achieve. Because the most unambiguous language available to us is that of mathematics, the trend has been toward more mathematical and hence provable methods of description (Woodcock and Loomes, 1988).

Perhaps the foremost barrier which prevents computer scientists from using mathematics for this purpose, however, is the common assignment statement. In a traditional programming language, a variable is a storage location that can be modified by such assignment statements. As a result of this, the meaning of a variable is position-dependent. To know what a variable stands for, it is necessary to know the precise point in the execution of a program about which an inquiry is made. This makes program verification by formal methods very difficult.

In contrast, a term in a declarative language has no computational history, but a definite value. This property is known as 'referential transparency'. A program is referentially transparent if it prohibits the assignment of different values to the same variable in the same run. Hence, although languages like PROLOG permit the use of variables, they require the program to be in effect rerun for each different value of the variable.

Languages characterised by referential transparency are known as declarative languages because, without assignments, programmers can declare only what effects should produce what outcomes. They do not need to prescribe the manner in which processing should occur.

**Advantages of the declarative approach**

The referential transparency property of declarative languages means that they have a number of advantages over conventional approaches (Eisenbach and Sadler, 1985):

1. Declarative languages stabilise variables so that mathematical techniques can be applied to fragments of code.
2. They serve to remove flow mechanisms such as loops and sequencing from explicit mention in the code.
3. This in turn enhances the possibility of parallel processing. Since any function in a program can be executed whenever all its inputs exist, rather than when the programmer decides that the processor is available for this purpose, there is no reason why a program cannot be spread over a number of separate processors.
4. In declarative languages the distinction between programs and data becomes blurred. This allows for the possibility of programs that are able to modify themselves in response to a changing environment.

The declarative approach also connects well with some of the logical modelling techniques, such as E–R diagrams and DFDs, that we have discussed. A DFD, for example, is a tool primarily for specifying the requirements of a problem declaratively. This declarative representation is then turned into some procedural code in traditional software development. Such a specification can however be used to represent directly the implementation of a system in declarative code. In this sense, the distinction between a specification of a problem and the program code begins to fade.

**Formal specification**

To illustrate some of the points made above, we now consider the process of formally specifying a piece of software as an example of the declarative approach. Formal specification is the specification of software through mathematics. This section considers the algebraic specification of a simple RDBMS (Gehani and McGettrick, 1986).

Algebraic specifications have two parts:

- The syntax which specifies the operations of the system.
- The semantics, in which a set of algebraic equations referred to as axioms relate the values created by the operations.

The formal specification for the RDBMS is:

```
1.   type database
     ----

2.   external operations new, add, empty, in, get
     --------  ----------
3.   internal operation insert
     --------  ---------

4.   syntax
     ------

5.   new: -> database
6.   add: database X name X relation -> database ∪ {ERROR}
7.   empty: database -> boolean
8.   in: database X name -> boolean
9.   delete: database X name -> database ∪ {ERROR}
10.  insert: database X name X relation -> database
11.  get: database X name -> relation ∪ {ERROR}
```

```
12. semantics
    ---------


13.   var d:database; n, m: name; r: relation
      ---


14.   axioms
      ------


15.       empty(new) = true
16.       empty(insert(d,n,r)) = false

17.       in(new,n) = false
18.       in(insert(d,m,r),n) = if n = m then true else in(d,n)

19.       delete(new,n) = ERROR
20.       delete(insert(d,m,r),n) = if n = m then d
                                    else insert(delete(d,n),m,r)

21.       get(new,n) = ERROR
22.       get(insert(d,m,r),n) = if n = m then r else get (d,n)

23.       add(d,n,r) = if in(d,n) then ERROR
                       else insert(d,n,r)

24. end database.
    ---
```

An informal interpretation of this specification is as follows:

line 1: indicates what is to be specified – database.
line 2: specifies the operations available to the users of the database.
line 3: specifies an operation internal to the database, that is, an operation not available to the user.
line 4: the start of the syntactic specifications.
line 5: specifies the syntax of the operation 'new'. Operation 'new ' takes no arguments and returns a value of type 'database'.
line 6: specifies that 'add' takes three arguments: a database, a name and a relation. It returns either a database or an error as its result.
line 12: the start of the semantic specifications.
line 13: variable d is declared to be of type 'database', n and m to be of type 'name', and r of type 'relation'.

line 15: the result of applying the operation 'empty' on a database that contains no relations is TRUE.

line 16: 'empty' returns FALSE if any relation has been inserted into a database.

line 17: the operation 'in' returns FALSE when one tries to see if a relation is present in an empty database.

line 18: operation 'in' checks to see if the relation named n is in the database by recursively looking at the relations inserted.

line 19: deleting a relation from an empty database results in an error.

line 20: a relation named n is deleted by recursively looking at all the relations inserted to see if it is present.

We can demonstrate the validity of the algebraic specification above by 'instantiating' the semantic equations with actual values. For example,

1. 'new' represents the empty database.
2. we add a relation r1 named SUPPLIER to an empty database:

```
add(new,SUPPLIER,r1) = insert(new,SUPPLIER,r1)
```

3. we add a relation r2 named PARTS to the database:

```
add(insert(new,SUPPLIER,r1),PARTS,r2) =

insert(insert(new,SUPPLIER,r1),PARTS,r2)
```

4. we check to see if a relation SHIPMENTS is in the database:

```
in(insert(insert(new,SUPPLIER,r1),PARTS,r2),SALES) =

in(insert(new,SUPPLIER,r1),SALES) =

in(new,SALES) =

false
```

## Conclusion

Conceptual modelling implies a leap to a more abstract level of system description. This leap is analogous to the one that has been achieved in moving from assembly languages to high-level programming languages or from piecemeal file structures to database systems. Each of these leaps stimulated the development of a whole range of new concepts, tools and techniques. The leap now needed for conceptual modelling requires high-level mechanisms for the specification of large, complex models of an organisation. It involves identifying concepts and establishing techniques for conceptual modelling. It will also involve developing tools (high-level languages, knowledge-based systems and advanced development environments etc.) with which to support these concepts and techniques.

Conceptual modelling in AI is knowledge representation. In database work it is semantic data modelling. In programming language research it is abstraction. The fundamental characteristic of this new level of system description represented by each of these endeavours is that it aims to be closer to the human conceptualisation of a domain of interest. Descriptions at this level will therefore enhance communication between system designers, domain experts and end-users. This will hopefully lead to a greater correspondence between user requirements and system implementation. Perhaps conceptual modelling may even solve some of the software problems with which we began this work.

# Bibliography

Maryam Alavi (1984). An Assessment of the Prototyping Approach to Information Systems Development. *CACM* **27** , pp. 556–573.

A. Al-Zobaidie and J.B. Grimson (1987). Expert Systems and Database Systems: How can They Serve Each Other? *Expert Systems* **4**, pp. 30–37.

D.E. Avison (1985). *Information Systems Development: a Database Approach*. Blackwell Scientific Publications, Oxford.

C.W. Bachmann (1969). Data Structure Diagrams. *Data Base* **1**, pp. 4–10.

C.W. Bachmann (1973). The Programmer as Navigator. *CACM* **16,** pp. 47–50.

F.T. Baker (1972). Chief Programmer Team Management of Production Programming. *IBM Systems Journal* **11**, pp. 57–73.

D. Benyon and S. Skidmore (1987). Towards a Toolkit for the Systems Analyst. *Computer Journal* **30**, pp. 2–7.

Paul Beynon-Davies (1987). Using Micro-based Expert System Shells. *Computing* 12 November, 1987

Paul Beynon-Davies (1988a). Intelligent Knowledge-based Systems and PICK (1). *ACCESS*.

Paul Beynon-Davies (1988b). Intelligent Knowledge-based Systems and PICK (2). *ACCESS*.

Paul Beynon-Davies (1988c). Frames and Relations. *Computing Techniques*.

British Computer Society (1976). Data Dictionary Systems Working Party Report.

N.D. Birrell and M.A. Ould (1985). *A Practical Handbook for Software Development*. Cambridge University Press.

Barry W. Boehm (1976). Software Engineering. *IEEE Transactions on Computers* C-25, pp. 1226–1241.

Barry W. Boehm (1981). *Software Engineering Economics*. Prentice-Hall, Englewood Cliffs, NJ.

Michael. H. Bracket (1987). *Developing Data Structured Databases*. Prentice-Hall, Englewood Cliffs, NJ. 1987.

M. L. Brodie, J. Mylopoulos, J. W. Schmidt (eds) (1984). *On Conceptual Modelling: perspectives from Artificial Intelligence, Databases and Programming Languages*. Springer-Verlag, Berlin.

F. P. Brooks (1975). *The Mythical Man-Month: Essays on Software Engineering*. Addison-Wesley, Reading, Mass.

P. P-S Chen (1976). *The Entity-Relationship Model – Toward a Unified View of Data. ACM Transactions on Database Systems* 1, pp. 9–36.

CODASYL (1971). Database Task Group.

E. F. Codd (1970). A Relational Model of Data for Large Shared Data Banks. *CACM* **13**, pp. 377–387.

E. F. Codd (1974). Recent Investigations into Relational Database Systems. *Proc. IFIP Congress.*

E. F. Codd (1985). Is Your Relational Database Management System really Relational? An Evaluation Scheme. ORACLE User's Conference.

Geoff Cutts (1987). *SSADM: Structured Systems Analysis and Design Methodology.* Paradigm, London.

C. J. Date (1986). *An Introduction to Database Systems*, Vol. 1, 4th edn. Addison-Wesley, Reading, Mass.

O. J. Dahl, E. W. Dijkstra, C. A. R. Hoare (1972). *Structured Programming.* Academic Press, New York.

A. Daniels and D. Yeates (1984). *Practical Systems Design.* Pitman, London.

P. A. Dearnley and P. J. Mayhew (1983). In Favour of System Prototypes and their Integration into the Systems Development Cycle. *The Computer Journal* **26**, pp. 36–42.

John K. Debenham (1988). Expert Systems: an Information Processing Perspective. In J. Ross Quinlan (ed.) *Applications of Expert Systems,* Addison-Wesley, Reading, Mass.

Tom De-Marco (1979a). *Structured Analysis and System Specification.* Prentice-Hall, Englewood Cliffs, NJ.

Tom De-Marco (1979b). *Concise Notes on Software Engineering.* Yourdon Press, New York.

Ed Downs, Peter Clare, and Ian Cole (1987). *Structured Systems Analysis and Design Method: Application and Context.* Prentice-Hall, Englewood Cliffs, NJ.

Tony Durham (1988). Putting some Muscle Behind a Glossy Front. *Computing* 28 January 1988.

S. Eisenbach and C. Sadler (1985). Declarative Languages: an overview. *BYTE* August 1985.

R. Fagin (1977). Multivalued Dependencies and a New Normal Form for Relational Databases. *ACM Trans. on Database Systems* 2.

R. Fagin (1979). Normal Forms and Relational Database Operators. *ACM SIGMOD Int. Symposium on Management of Data*, pp. 153–60.

Edward. A. Feigenbaum (1977). The Art of Artificial Intelligence: themes and case studies of knowledge engineering. *International Joint Conference on Artificial Intelligence* 5, pp 1014–1029.

Edward. A. Feigenbaum and Pamela Mccorduck (1984). *The Fifth Generation: AI and Japan's Computer Challenge to the World.* Michael Joseph, London.

P. Feldman and D. Miller (1986). Entity Model Clustering: Structuring a Data Model by Abstraction. *The Computer Journal* 29, pp. 348–360.

G. Fitzgerald, N. Stokes and J. R. G. Wood (1985). Feature Analysis of Contemporary Information Systems Methodologies. *The Computer Journal* 28, pp. 223–30.

N. Gehani and A. D. McGettrick (1986). *Software Specification Techniques.* Addison-Wesley, Reading, Mass.

Chris Gane and Trish Sarson (1977). *Structured Systems Analysis: Tools and Techniques.* Prentice-Hall, Englewood Cliffs, NJ.

J. Gaschnig (1982). Prospector: an Expert System for Mineral Exploitation. In A.Bond (ed). *Machine Intelligence,* Infotech State of the Art Report 9.

Richard. V. Giddings (1984). Accommodating Uncertainty in Software Design. *CACM* 27, pp. 428–34.

Mark. L. Gillenson (1987). The Duality of Database Structures and Design Techniques. *CACM* 30, pp. 1056–65.

Alex Goodall (1983). *The Guide to Expert Systems.* Learned Information, Oxford.

I. T. Hawryszkiewicz (1988). *Introduction to Systems Analysis and Design.* Prentice-Hall, Englewood Cliffs, NJ.

D. R. Howe (1983). *Data Analysis for Database Design.* Edward Arnold, London.

M. A. Jackson (1984). *Principles of Program Design.* Academic Press, New York.

Matthias Jarke and Yannis Vassilou (1984). Coupling Expert Systems with Database Management Systems. In Reitman (1984).

Rory Johnston (1986). Early Applications Get User Approval. *Expert Systems User,* Nov. 1986.

Russell Jones (1987). Business gets on the Trail of Expert Advice. *Computing.* 10 December

L. Kerschberg (1987a). Expert Database Systems. *Computer Bulletin.* June.

L. Kerschberg (1987b). *Expert Database Systems: Proceedings from the 1st International Conference.* Benjamin Cummins.

David King (1984). *Current Practices in Software Development: a Guide to Successful Systems.* Yourdon Press, New York.

M. J. King and J. Pardoe (1985). *Program Design Using JSP: A Practical Introduction.* Macmillan, London.

William Kent (1983). A Simple Guide to Five Normal Forms in Relational Database Theory. *CACM* 26, pp. 120–5.

Brian W. Kernighan and P. J. Plauger (1976). *Software Tools*. Addison-Wesley, Reading, Mass.

H. K. Klein and R. A. Hirscheim (1987). A Comparative Framework of Data Modeling Paradigms and Approaches. *The Computer Journal* **30**, pp. 8–15.

Robert Kowalski. Algorithm = logic + control. *CACM* **22**, pp. 424–436.

Robert Kowalski (1979). *Logic for Problem-Solving*. North-Holland, Amsterdam.

J. W. Lloyd (1983). An Introduction to Deductive Database Systems. *Australian Computer Journal* **15**, pp. 52–7.

R. N. Maddison and A. J. Gawronski (1985). A Data Dictionary for Learning Data Analysis. *The Computer Journal* **28**, pp. 270–1.

Tracey Maney and Ian Reid (1986). *A Management Guide to Artifical Intelligence*. Paradigm, London.

James Martin (1982). *Strategic Data-Planning Methodologies*. Prentice-Hall, Englewood Cliffs, NJ.

James Martin (1984). *An Information Systems Manifesto*. Prentice-Hall, Englewood Cliffs, NJ.

James Martin and Carma McClure (1985). *Diagramming Techniques for Analysts and Programmers*. Prentice-Hall, Englewood Cliffs, NJ.

Pamela Mccorduck (1978). *Machines who Think*. Freeman, San Francisco.

J. McDermid (Ed.) (1985). *Integrated Project Support Environments*. Peter Peregrinus Ltd, London.

J. McDermott (1980). R1: an expert in the computer systems domain. *Proceedings of American Association for AI Conference*.

Brian Meek, Patricia Heath, and Nick Rushby (1983). *Guide to Good Programming Practice*. 2nd Edn. Ellis-Horwood, Chichester.

George. A. Miller (1967). The Magical Number Seven, Plus or Minus Two: Some Limits on our Capacity for Processing Information. In *The Psychology of Communication: Seven Essays*. Penguin, London.

ORACLE (1984). ORACLE Overview and Introduction to SQL.

M. Page-Jones (1980). *The Practical Guide to Structured Systems Design*. Yourdon Press, New York.

Joan Peckham and Fred Maryanski (1988). Semantic Data Models. *ACM Computing Surveys* **20**, pp. 153–89.

W. Reitman (1984). *Artificial Intelligence Applications for Business*. Ablex Publishing, California.

K. A. Robinson (1979). An Entity/Event Data Modelling Method. *The Computer Journal* **22**, pp. 270–81.

R. Rock-Evans (1981). *Data Analysis*. A Computer Weekly Publication, IPC Business Press, London.

C. J. Rosenquist (1982). Entity Life Cycle Models and their Applicability to Information Systems Development Life Cycles. *The Computer Journal* **25**, pp. 307–15.

P. Russell, A. Bracher (1986). An Integrated Knowledge Representation Scheme for Expert Database Systems. *2nd International Expert Systems Conference.*

P. W. Sellars (1985). IPSEs in Commercial Data Processing. In J. Mcdermid.

M. J. R. Shave (1981). Entities, Functions and Binary Relations: steps to a conceptual schema. *The Computer Journal* **24**.

M. Shaw (1984). The Impact of Modelling and Abstraction Concerns on Modern Programming Languages. In Brodie *et al.*, (1984).

E. H. Shortliffe (1976). *Computer-based Medical Consultations: MYCIN.* Elsevier, Amsterdam.

Barry. G. Silverman (Ed) (1987). *Expert Systems for Business.* Addison-Wesley, Reading, Mass.

R. A. Snowdon, N. C. Munro, N. W. Davis, M. I. Jackson (1985). Advanced Support Environments: an industry viewpoint. In J. Mcdermid (ed). *Integrated Project Support Environments.* Peter Peregrinus.

J. F. Sowa (1984). *Conceptual Structures: Information Processing in Mind and Machine.* Addison-Wesley, Reading, Mass.

Michael Stonebraker and Lawrence. A. Rowe (1985). The Design of Postgress. Memorandum, Electronics Research Laboratory, University of California, Berkeley.

D. Tsitchizris and F. Lochovsky (1982). *Data Models.* Prentice-Hall, Englewood Cliffs, NJ.

A. Underwood (1984). DFD's or Plain English? *Proceedings of the Australian Computer Conference.* Sydney.

M. Vetter (1987). *Strategy for Data Modelling.* Wiley, New York.

Adrian Walker (1981). Databases, Expert Systems, and PROLOG. In Reitman (1984).

J. Warnier (1971). *Logical Construction of Systems.* Van Nostrand, Princeton, NJ.

Anthony. I. Wasserman and Steven Gutz (1982). The Future of Programming. *CACM* **25**, pp. 196–206.

G. M. Weinberg (1971). *The Psychology of Computer Programming.* Van Nostrand, Princeton, NJ.

Victor Weinberg (1980). *Structured Analysis.* Prentice-Hall, Englewood Cliffs, NJ.

A. T. Wood-Harper and G. Fitzgerald (1982). A Taxonomy of Current Approaches to Systems Analysis. *The Computer Journal* **25**, pp. 12–16.

Patrick Henry Winston and Karen A. Prendergast (Eds.) (1984). *The AI Business: the Commercial Uses of Artificial Intelligence*. MIT Press, Cambridge, Mass.

J. Woodcock and M. Loomes (1988). *Software Engineering Mathematics*. Pitman, London.

Edward Yourdon (1988). *Structured Walkthroughs*. Yourdon Press, New York.

Edward Yourdon and Larry. L. Constantine (1979). *Structured Design: Fundamentals of a Discipline of Computer Program and System Design*. Prentice-Hall, Englewood Clffs, NJ.

# *Glossary*

Attribute   The property of an entity. A column in a table.

Balancing   Ensuring that the symbols at various levels in a DFD hierarchy match.

Black box   A highly cohesive model that can be used to build low-coupled systems.

Boyce–Codd Rule   Every determinant must be the primary key of a table.

CASE (Computer-Aided Software Engineering)   *See* IPSE, 4GL.

Cohesion   A function of how closely the elements within a single module are related to one another.

Conceptual modelling   The modelling of the real world for information systems development. Associated primarily with E–R diagramming.

Coupling   A measure of the degree of interdependence between modules.

Data analysis   A general term for E–R diagramming and normalisation.

Database   A centralised pool of organisational data.

Data flow   A pipeline of data.

Data dictionary   A repository of metadata.

Data modelling   *See* data analysis.

DBMS (Database Management System)   A system which manages all interactions within a database.

DFD (Data-Flow Diagram)   A diagrammatic representation of information flow.

Data store   A repository of data.

Decision table   A matrix-like representation for process logic.

Decision tree   A hierarchical representation for process logic.

Declarative language   A language which displays referential transparency.

Degree   The cardinality of a relationship: 1:1, 1:$M$, $M$:$N$.

**Dependency**   The reverse of determinancy.

**Determinancy**   The association between attributes in a table.

**Determinancy diagram**   A diagrammatic representation of the determinancy in a table.

**Domain**   The range of possible values for an attribute.

**E–R (Entity–Relationship) diagram**   A representation of real-world entities and relationships.

**Entity**   A thing which the enterprise recognises as having an independent existence and which can be uniquely identified.

**Entity life-history**   A representation of the flow of events affecting an entity.

**Entity life-history matrix**   A matrix which plots entities against events.

**External entity**   Something, lying outside the context of a system, which is the net originator or receiver of system data.

**Fourth-generation language (4GL)**   A language in which the programmer is able to specify logic without needing to detail aspects of control.

**Fourth-generation environment**   A term for a package made up of a fourth-generation language and an RDBMS.

**Formal methods**   The application of mathematics to information systems specification.

**Imperative language**   A language which does not display referential transparency.

**Information centre (IC)**   A centre of information engineering excellence.

**Information engineering**   A global concern with the management of information in organisations.

**Information resource management (IRM)**   The process of building and managing a corporate information architecture.

**IPSE (Integrated Project Support Environment)**   A total working environment for the professional software engineer.

**JSP (Jackson Structured Programming)**   A method of data-directed program design.

**KBS (Knowledge Based System)**   A system of facts and rules.

Levelling    Representing an information system as a partitioned hierarchy of DFDs.

Logical DFD    A DFD abstracted from physical details.

LSDM (Learmonth and Burchett System Design Method)    A commercial product similar to SSADM.

Membership class    The participation of each entity in a relationship.

Module    *See* black box.

Normalisation    *See* TNF data analysis.

Optionality    *See* membership class.

Physical DFD    A representation of physical information flow.

Process    A transformation of incoming data flow into outgoing data flow.

Process description    A description of process logic.

Production rule    An IF–THEN construct used to represent chunks of knowledge in a KBS.

Prototyping    The production of software as a means of determining user requirements.

Pseudo-code    *See* structured English.

Referential transparency    A program is referentially transparent if it prohibit assigning different values to the same variable in the same run.

Relation    A constrained table.

Relational database    A database of relations.

Relationship    An association between two or more entities.

Sink    *See* external entity.

Software engineering    The systematic application of a set of appropriate techniques to the entire project life cycle.

Source    *See* external entity.

SSADM (Structured Systems Analysis and Design Method)    A UK Government standard methodology.

Strategic data planning    *See* IRM.

Structured analysis    An attempt to separate the logical from the physical description of information systems.

**Structure chart**   A diagrammatic representation of a hierarchy of program modules.

**Structured design**   A term used by Yourdon and Constantine to include their discussion of coupling, cohesion and the derivation of structure charts.

**Structure diagram**   A graphic technique for representing process and data structures in JSP.

**Structured English**   A subset of English used for process description.

**Structured programming**   A disciplined programming methodology based on firm notions of an appropriate syntax for procedural programming languages.

**Structured walkthrough**   A group review of any product of the development process prior to its release.

**Table**   A simple representation for data files. *See* relation.

**Third-generation language**   Languages such as COBOL or C in which logic is embedded within control structures.

**TNF (Third Normal Form) data analysis**   A step-by-step technique for transforming data subject to a whole range of update anomalies into an organised database free from such problems.

**Tuple**   A row in a relation.

# *Suggested Solutions*

**Chapter 4**

1. Normalisation is a technique for transforming data subject to a whole range of update anomalies into an organised database free from such problems.
2. Unwanted side-effects evident in an unnormalised database.
3. Removes repeating groups.
4. Removes part-key dependencies.
5. Removes inter-data and inter-key dependencies.
6. More systematic. Easier to apply and understand. Being diagrammatic it is less prone to error.
7.

```
Doctor(Doctor_no, Doctor_name)
       ---------

   Patient(Patient_no, Patient_name, Date_of_admission)
           ----------

   Schedule(Doctor_no, Operation_no)
            ---------  -------------

   Operation(Operation_no, Operation_date, Operation_time,
             ------------

             Patient_no)
```

This is an interesting problem in that it highlights that when we use such phrases as 'A determines B' and 'B is dependent on A' we should really say 'A functionally determines B' and 'B is functionally dependent on A'. An appropriate set of tables for the schedule database is given above. Note that although we cannot say that A functionally determines B and vice versa, we can say that A and B are non-functionally dependent since there is an evident association between these two attributes. In determinancy diagram terms this is represented by a box drawn around both attributes.

8.

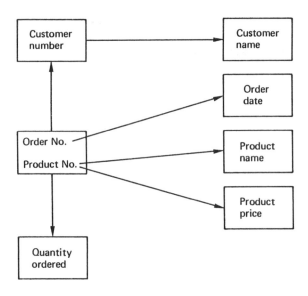

## Chapter 5

1. Person–Grade, Person–Position, Position–Department, Department–Position.
2.

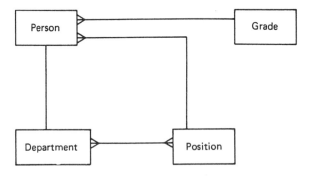

3. The many-to-many relationship between department and position which appears to be a direct representation of the relationships between person and position, and person and department.
4. E–R diagram of sales database in chapter 13.

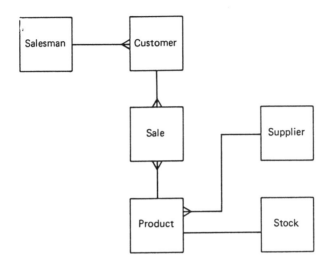

## Chapter 6

1. Try rereading the chapter on databases and database management systems, particularly the section on program-data independence.
2.

- Two-dimensional interconnection is more easily shown on a diagram.
- Descriptive information is included in the symbols of a diagram. Diagrams then require less effort to produce; are easier to under-stand; and much more concise.
- Rough versions of diagrams are easily made.
- Data-flow diagrams can be used to show progressive levels of detail.

3(a) This DFD does not tell you much. The data-flow names and process name are too general to be useful.

(b) Two problems: first, an unlabelled DFD; second, the process does not seem to be doing much to the transaction flow.

4. Besides the flow and process names being unmeaningful, levels 1 and 2 do not balance. H goes into process 1.2 and comes out again. Flow E is nowhere to be seen on level 2.

5. The flow of time sheets in a payroll system might be represented as:

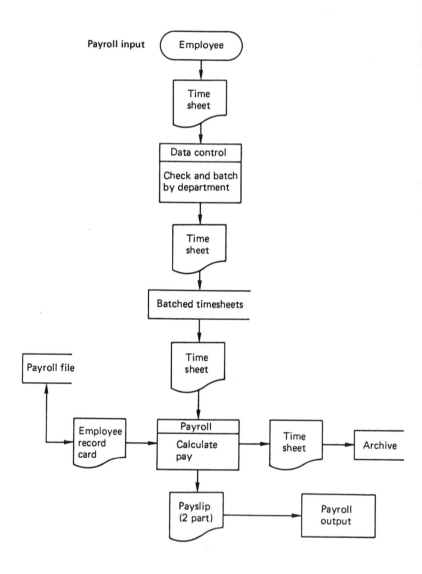

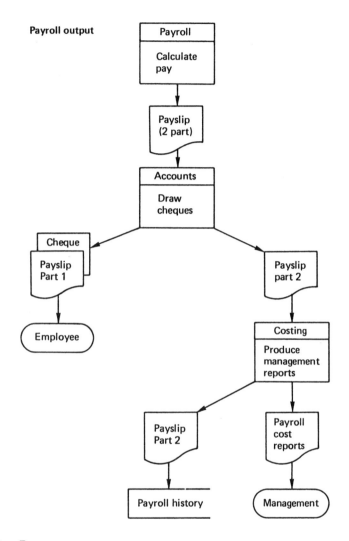

## Chapter 7

1.

```
PROCESSES
    Check credit status
    Determine discount
    Create purchase order
    Despatch goods
```

```
FLOWS

    Sales order
    Prepayment request
    Validated sales order
    Discounted sales order
    Order information
    Credit status
    Customer status
    Goods information
    Purchase order
    Bulk supplies
    Delivery note
    Wholesaler invoice
    Goods
    Shipping note
    FF invoice

STORES

    Retailers
    Sales orders
    Goods
```

2.

```
FF INVOICE = INVOICE NO + CUSTOMER NAME + CUSTOMER ADDRESS +
                (DESPATCH DATE) + {PRODUCT NO + PRODUCT
                DESCRIPTION + QTY ORDERED + UNIT PRICE + ORDER
                VALUE} + TOTAL VALUE
                * Invoice sent to retailer with shipping note
                and goods *
```

3.

```
PROCESS NAME: Depatch Goods

INBOUND        Bulk supplies, delivery note, wholesaler
DATA FLOWS:    invoice

OUTBOUND       Goods, shipping note, FF invoice
DATA FLOWS:
```

4. The sign '+' is not a summation operator. It is a concatenation operator. Hence:

    10 = 5 + 5   wrong
    55 = 5 + 5   right

# Chapter 8

1.

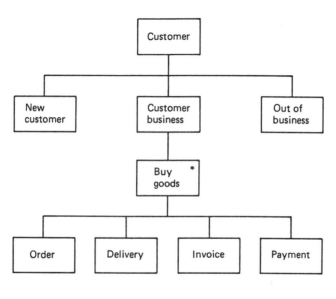

2.

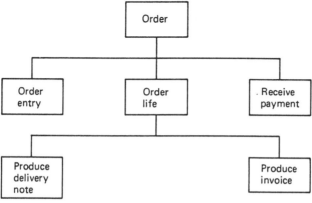

3.

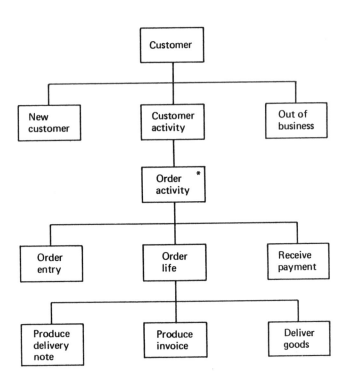

4.

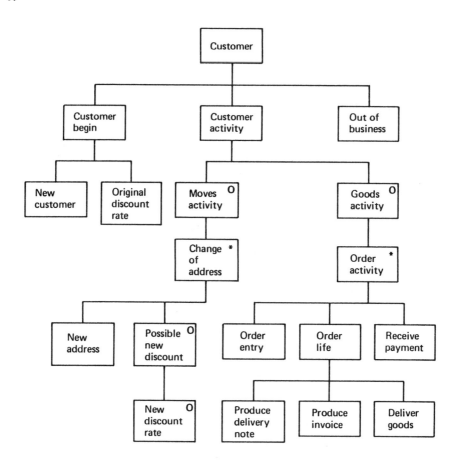

## Chapter 9

1. There are two possible meanings:
   - 'Customers with more than £1000 in their deposit account and an average current account balance exceeding £100 *or* persons who have been customers for more than 5 years'.
   - 'Customers with more than £1000 in their deposit account *and* persons with an average current account balance exceeding £100 pounds or who have been customers for more than 5 years'.

2.

```
IF deposit_balance GT 1000
     AND average_current_balance GT 100
   THEN customer is entitled to free banking

   IF customer has been with the bank for more than 5 years
   THEN customer is entitled to free banking

   IF deposit_balance GT 1000
   THEN customer is entitled to free banking

   IF average_current_balance GT 100
    OR customer has been with the bank for more than 5 years
   THEN customer is entitled to free banking
```

3. Unambiguous. Logic is more clearly laid out. A step closer to program code.

4(a)

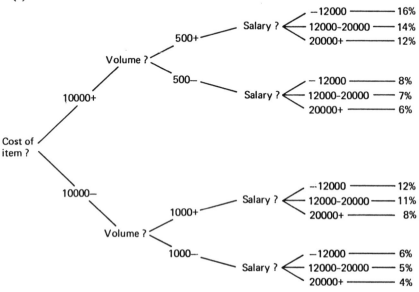

4(b)

```
Condition Stub:                          Condition Entry:
-------------------------------------------------------------------
ITEM COST      10+ 10+ 10+ 10+ 10+ 10+ 10- 10- 10- 10- 10- 10-
VOLUME OF SALE 5+  5+  5+  -5  -5  -5  10+ 10+ 10+ 10- 10- 10-
SALARY         -12 -20 20+ -12 -20 20+ -12 -20 20+ -12 -20 20+
-------------------------------------------------------------------
Action Stub:                             Action Entry:
-------------------------------------------------------------------
16%             X
14%                 X
12%                     X               X
11%                                         X
8%                          X                   X
7%                              X
6%                                  X               X
5%                                                      X
4%                                                          X
-------------------------------------------------------------------
```

5. It depends by whom it is used. Generally the decision table is more
   economical and less redundant.

6.

```
CASE one-to-one relationship
     AND memberclass of both entities is mandatory
     BEGIN
        create one table to hold both entities
     END

CASE one-to-one relationship
     AND memberclass of one entity is optional
     BEGIN
        create two tables
        post ID from mandatory table to optional table
     END
```

```
CASE one-to-one relationship
    AND memberclass of both entities is optional
    BEGIN
        create three tables
        one for each entity and one for the relationship
        post IDs from entity tables to relationship table
    END
CASE one-to-many relationship
    AND memberclass of many entity is mandatory
    BEGIN
        create two tables
        post ID from one end to many end of relationship
    END
CASE one-to-many relationship
    AND memberclass of both entities is optional
    BEGIN
        create three tables
        one for each entity and one for the relationship
        post IDs from entity tables to relationship table
    END
CASE many-to-many relationship
    BEGIN
        create three tables
        one for each entity and one for the relationship
        post IDs from entity tables to relationship table
    END
ENDCASE
```

## Chapter 10

1(a) A flowchart shows the sequence of steps to be executed. A structure chart shows hierarchy of functions.
 (b) A begins, A calls B, B begins, B calls C, C begins, C completes, C returns to B, B completes, B returns to A, A completes.

2.

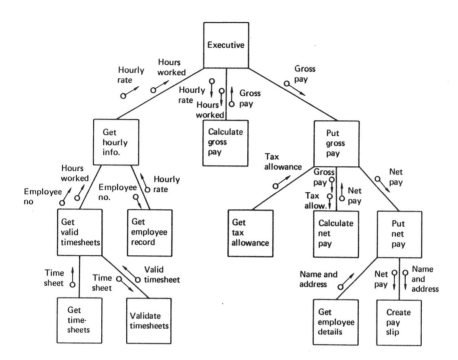

# *Index*